Spiritual Pilgrims

CARL JUNG
AND
TERESA OF AVILA

JOHN WELCH, O. CARM.

PAULIST PRESS
New York/Ramsey

The Publisher gratefully acknowledges the use of the following materials: Selections from *Memories, Dreams, Reflections,* by C.G. Jung, recorded and edited by Aniela Jaffe, translated by Richard and Clara Winston. Copyright © 1963 by Random House, Inc., and reprinted by permission of Pantheon Books, a Division of Random House, Inc.; excerpts from *The Collected Works of St. Teresa of Avila* Vol. 1, translated by Kieran Kavanaugh and Otilio Rodriguez, Copyright © 1976 by Washington Province of Discalced Carmelites, Inc. and reprinted by permission of ICS Publications, Washington, D.C.; selections from the following volumes are all reprinted by permission of Princeton University Press: *The Collected Works of C.G. Jung,* trans. R.F.C. Hull, Bollingen Series XX. Vol. 1: *Psychiatric Studies,* copyright © 1957, 1970 by Princeton University Press; *The Collected Works of C.G. Jung,* trans. R.F.C. Hull, Bollingen Series XX. Vol. 2: *Experimental Researches,* copyright © 1973 by Princeton University Press; *The Collected Works of C.G. Jung,* trans. R.F.C. Hull, Bollingen Series XX. Vol. 4: *Freud and Psychoanalysis,* copyright © 1961 by Princeton University Press; *The Collected Works of C.G. Jung,* trans. R.F.C. Hull, Bollingen Series XX. Vol. 5: *Symbols of Transformation,* copyright © 1956 by Princeton University Press; *The Collected Works of C.G. Jung,* trans. R.F.C. Hull, Bollingen Series XX. Vol. 6: *Psychological Types,* copyright © 1971 by Princeton University Press; *The Collected Works of C.G. Jung,* trans. R.F.C. Hull, Bollingen Series XX. Vol. 7: *Two Essays on Analytical Psychology,* copyright 1953, © 1966 by Princeton University Press; *The Collected Works of C.G. Jung,* trans. R.F.C. Hull, Bollingen Series XX. Vol. 8: *The Structure and Dynamics of the Psyche,* copyright © 1960, 1969 by Princeton University Press; *The Collected Works of C.G. Jung,* trans. R.F.C. Hull, Bollingen Series XX. Vol. 9, I, *The Archetypes and the Collective Unconscious,* copyright © 1959, 1969 by Princeton University Press; *The Collected Works of C.G. Jung,* trans. R.F.C. Hull, Bollingen Series XX, Vol. 9, II, *Aion: Researches into the Phenomenology of the Self,* copyright © 1959 by Princeton University Press; *The Collected Works of C.G. Jung,* trans. R.F.C. Hull, Bollingen Series XX. Vol. 10: *Civilization in Transition,* copyright © 1964, 1970 by Princeton University Press; *The Collected Works of C.G. Jung,* trans. R.F.C. Hull, Bollingen Series XX. Vol. 11: *Psychology and Religion: West and East,* copyright © 1958, 1969 by Princeton University Press; *The Collected Works of C.G. Jung,* trans. R.F.C.

Contents

to my family,
JOHN AND MYRA WELCH

and to
MY CARMELITE BROTHERS AND SISTERS

*I would like to express my gratitude
and deep appreciation for the encouragement
and support of the following people in writing this book:
Ernest Larkin, Vivian Whitehead,
Thomas O'Meara, Donald Buggert, Leo McCarthy
and the community of
Whitefriars Hall, Washington, D.C.*

FOREWORD

Throughout the North American continent there is growing interest in the spiritual journey. I find it everywhere I go. I talk with spiritually hungry people from all religious backgrounds and I hear again and again the cry for adequate spiritual guides and for books which can lead us upon the spiritual way. John Welch has written one of the finest guidebooks of the spiritual journey I have encountered within the field. It speaks to age-old needs with a new language that can reach modern seekers.

Although the book purports to be a study of the psychology of Carl Jung and the spirituality of Teresa of Avila, it is far more. It is a personal journey into one of the most important writings of St. Teresa, *The Interior Castle*, on which the author was given great help through an understanding of the human psyche and soul provided by the great psychiatrist. We are given the impression that the author has made that journey and is beckoning to us to come on the way with him. Baron Von Hugel showed that the only way to study mysticism was to study mystics and then follow their example. Fr. Welch has done just that. He has looked at the lives and writing of two people who have spent their entire lives on the religious quest into their own interior castles. He shows clearly the dangers which beset the traveler on this inner journey and he provides a clear image of the goal of the journey which spurs us to make the voyage.

I have been reading books by Jung and about Jung for thirty years. The understanding of Jung provided by the author is one of the most sensitive and sympathetic I have encountered. Without giving way to sentimentality or dodging any of the important deficiencies of Jung, Welch provides the picture of a person who knew the human soul in its heights and depths, one who kept relentlessly on the journey for over fifty years. This struggle resulted in the development of a new language by which the deepest levels of the psyche could be described more accurately than ever before. This virtue alone makes this book one of the best studies of the religious significance of Jung and of his Christian significance in particular.

Teresa of Avila made an incredible impression on her time

and upon the life of the Catholic Church. However, few twenti-
eth-century pilgrims have been able to feel the impact of her understanding of the human soul and the religious way. Her
language is the language of sixteenth-century Spain which was
just emerging from the Middle Ages. Without avoiding the
problems surrounding Teresa or the fact that some of her convents were built on the spoils of the New World, Welch provides a living picture of this great woman and her inner
journey; it is a journey which reveals the nature of the journey
that many of us are destined to make. Teresa speaks of eternal
realities that are confirmed in the experiences and writings of
Jung.

One of the basic unrealities of most accounts of the inner
journey is that they avoid discussing the almost intolerable difficulties we often encounter on this heroic way. I have discovered
no better analysis of these roadblocks and hindrances than the
chapter entitled "Serpents and Devils in the Shadows." This
should be required reading for all spiritual guides and those
who venture inward. The darkness is real, and those prepared to
meet it have the best chance of passing through the abyss successfully. No existentialist ever described the difficulties more
adequately.

Describing an adequate goal for the human quest is a difficult undertaking. At this point Jung sometimes appears to be far
removed from the Christian way. Welch shows the ambiguities
of Jung's final answer and how close the latest strand of Jung's
thought and experience is to that of St. Teresa. Drawing on Sebastian Moore and William Thompson he provides a bridge between Jung, St. Teresa and the most authentic Christian
experience. The final answer to evil is only found in the resurrection of the Crucified One who has met evil and death and has
conquered. The resurrected Risen Christ is our final goal, our
hope that we can make it through to wholeness, and our companion on that way. And the evidence that we have touched this
goal is found in the quality of loving concern for those around
us in every station of life.

Morton Kelsey

INTRODUCTION

This book is an attempt to help the reader live a fully human yet spiritual life. Its premise is that God calls us into life and into the fullness of our personhood. Centering our life on God does not rob us of our personality but guarantees it. This book is about Christian individuation, the movement into the wholeness of one's personality as union with God deepens.

Two sources are fundamental to this study. One source is Carl Jung's depth psychology which is a reflection upon contemporary human experience. The other source is *The Interior Castle*, a work by Teresa of Avila, a sixteenth century Spanish Carmelite nun.

Both Carl Jung and Teresa of Avila were perceptive observers of human interiority. Teresa wrote about the soul, the human person in his or her relationship to God. Jung studied the psyche and the relationship of the person to his or her own depths. Each illumines our interiority but from a different perspective. Studying them together heightens their helpfulness.

Images abound in the works of both authors. Teresa expressed her growing relationship to God in rich imagery. And Jung saw images as expressions of deep human experience. Image is a key for entering their writings.

Jung theorized that the deepest part of the psyche was transpersonal, a common possession of all humanity. This "collective unconscious" is composed of archetypes which are potential patternings for the development of personality. The archetypes are seeds of the self, sources of energy available for an individual's growth into wholeness.

Since the archetypes are unconscious they cannot be known directly. They are experienced through symbols which express the archetypes and make their energy available for integration into conscious personality. Jung believed that the psyche expresses depth experiences first of all in images which are symbolic expressions of the experiences, and then in concepts which represent a secondary-level thinking. Teresa Avila's work is an example of this process.

The Interior Castle is a classic in the Christian mystical tradition and in Spanish literature. In this work, Teresa of Avila describes the journey of a "soul" from the outer environs of a castle to its center where the King lives. She is describing her own prayer experiences which involved a series of transformations culminating in a spiritual union with Christ. She encourages the reader to enter within the castle of the soul and travel to God at the center.

The journey involves passing through six "dwelling places" (or "mansions") before arriving at the center, the seventh dwelling place. Teresa's unique castle is global and so the dwelling places are similar to spheres within spheres which enfold the center like the leaves of a palm. Each dwelling place consists of many rooms, arranged above, below, and to the side of one another.

The journey to the center has two movements which Teresa likens to the efforts involved in filling two troughs of water. The prayer in the first three dwelling places is an active prayer of meditation. It is likened to arduously filling a trough of water from a distant source through a series of aqueducts. The prayer in the last three dwelling places is a receptive prayer of contemplation. It is likened to a trough easily filling with water because it is located at the source. The middle dwelling place, the fourth, is a transitional situation.

The work is highly imaginative. The castle is the dominant image but within it are numerous other images presenting a theater within a theater. Among the major images are castle, water, journey, serpents, devils, butterfly, marriage and Christ.

Teresa has been called a psychological mystic because the journey to God, for her, is also a journey to the self. It is an inward journey to God which is, at the same time, a movement into self-knowledge. Union with God at the center involves the fullest possession of one's life. Teresa is a sensitive observer of human interiority and her writing attempts to convey the experience of a growing union with God.

This present study examines the psychological dimension of Teresa's travel through the castle. Her subtle descriptions of inner experiences provide a topography of human development, which is at the same time religious conversion.

In accord with Jung's theory, I am hypothesizing that Teresa's images are the primary expression of her inner experiences. Her commentary on her experiences, then, is a secondary mode of communication. Her images are symbols, pregnant expressions of meanings which can only partially be articulated.

The images in *The Interior Castle* become vehicles for entering more deeply into Teresa's experiences. And because the images express collective depths, they become vehicles for the reader's entry into her or his own archetypal depths. In other words, Teresa's images tell not only her story, but the story of the human psyche.

Jung explored many of the images, or images similar to them, which can be found in *The Interior Castle*. He discussed their typical meaning when used as symbols of depth experiences.

After an introductory chapter on images, each chapter of this work focuses on one of Teresa's images. The human experience captured by that symbol is discussed and Jung's psychological findings are related to it. His observations help explore the experience expressed in the image. I then demonstrate how and where Teresa uses the image in *The Interior Castle*. And finally, the dialogue between the two authors, through the juxtaposition of their writings, leads to reflections, understandings, and practices which, hopefully, will enhance Christian living.

The following is a brief summary of Jung's findings as they relate to Teresa's images:

Castle   As Teresa described it, the castle gives the appearance of a mandala figure, a circular symbol of the self, the goal of psychological development.

Water · It is a favorite image of Teresa's. Jung found that water was the most common symbol for the unconscious.

Journey · The movement through the dwelling places has remarkably similar contours to the individuation process, Jung's description of human development.

Serpents · They are Teresa's image for outer collective forces which hinder the inward journey. Jung found that such images also represent inner collective forces. They nourish the individual when consciously appropriated, but they are potentially destructive when lived out unconsciously.

Devils · Devils are one of the personifications of the neglected, inferior side of the personality which Jung called the shadow. He encouraged recognition and acceptance of this shadow side.

Butterfly · It is Teresa's image of dying and rising in union with Christ. Jung saw the image used as an allegory of the psyche as the self emerges through a series of transformations. The butterfly expresses the healing power of the psyche.

Marriage · Teresa's image represents the intimacy of the spiritual union with God. Jung saw masculine and feminine as a basic polarity in human existence expressing the experience of "otherness." At the same time this polarity demonstrates a dynamic movement toward unity and wholeness both within the individual and in human communities.

Christus Jung maintained that he could not differentiate symbols for self from symbols for God. Psychologically, Christ is a powerful symbol of the self. But Jung was critical of the Christ image because it contained no shadow side. Christ crucified between two thieves was a more complete image of the self, according to Jung.

In the beginning of his autobiography Carl Jung states: "Thus it is that I have now undertaken, in my eighty-third year, to tell my personal myth. I can only make direct statements, only 'tell stories.' Whether or not the stories are 'true' is not the problem. The only question is whether what I tell is *my* fable, *my* truth." In this study I conclude that Teresa of Avila, in her sixty-second year, told her personal myth, her symbols-in-narrative. *The Interior Castle* is a document of Christian individuation.

Teresa's writing indicates that religious conversion effects psychological transformations. She also suggests that successful negotiations of life-passages should result in deeper religious commitments.

The Interior Castle is an example of story-telling. The process which it suggests is the imaging of experience for the communicating and appropriating of that experience. As we tell our story we become that story. As we become aware of our depth experiences through their symbolic expression, and hear God's call in them, we are challenged to respond.

CHAPTER ONE

Finding Images For Our Story

We can grow in awareness of the images which deeply affect us in our lives. They can be discovered, listened to, and incorporated into our ongoing story. In our dreams, in our loves, on our journeys, we are being addressed by images. They are inviting us to enter more deeply into our lives, to allow our stories to unfold.

This chapter contains an introduction to Jung's theories concerning the relationship of images to the unconscious. In particular, the images resulting from dreams, projections, and feelings are discussed. The chapter also includes a summary of *The Interior Castle* and a discussion of Teresa of Avila's use of imagery. This discussion leads to an examination of the place of image in religious experience, especially in the difficult times of transformation.

Carl Jung's Work with Images

The studies of Carl Jung led him to understand that the human psyche thinks, primarily, in images. Images are a natural language for the psyche. Only secondarily do we move to conceptual thought. So, for example, the images in dreams are not a code developed by the psyche to hide its real thoughts. The images of the dream are the thought, in the natural undisguised language of the psyche. We have forgotten how to read that language.

Jung was convinced that we express our fundamental meanings in image, image which is symbolic of these meanings. And he urged us to look at the images in our lives in a symbolic way so that they may reveal to us our deeper meanings, our fuller selves. He came to respect the power of images in human living through his personal experience.

Jung was born in Switzerland in 1875. From an early age he was particularly susceptible to dream and fantasy images. These realms of his psyche he came to call his "number two personality." This personality in time became more familiar to him through his studies of the unconscious.

He finished medical school and entered psychiatric studies in 1900, the year Freud published *The Interpretation of Dreams*. These two pioneers in psychology eventually became good friends. Jung developed a private practice and combined it with an academic post.

Through a series of disagreements and disillusionments, Jung and Freud parted company. Shortly thereafter, in 1914, Jung resigned his post at the University of Zurich and also resigned as president of the International Psychoanalytical Association. These events signaled a general withdrawal from the larger social world and outer activities. He entered a long period of crisis, of inner turmoil.

For a renewal of his life he felt that he needed to face his inner dream and fantasy images. He needed to integrate his "number two personality" into his life. This period of time, 1913–1919, Jung discusses in his autobiography in the chapter titled, "Confrontations with the Unconscious."[1]

His inner world proved to be a cosmos as large as the outer world. Jung's explorations of this world in these years have provided a mapping for others to follow. It was in these explorations that Jung came to realize the tendency of the psyche to speak in images. Jung had to learn this language. "The years when I was pursuing my inner images," he wrote, "were the most important in my life—in them everything essential was decided. It all began then; the later details are only supplements and clarifications of the material that burst forth from the un-conscious, and at first swamped me. It was the *prima materia* for a lifetime's work."[2]

Jung emerged from this period of time with his distinctive theories in place. He published the results in two papers which were revised and published as *Two Essays on Analytical Psychology.* In another work, *Psychological Types,* he defined his basic con-cepts and terms. His further works deepened and extended these theories.

Jung's work with his inner images was a grand experiment. He had to experiment with locating his images, listening to them, and deriving meaning from them for his life. He basically sought an integration of his life and saw the images as clues to the unlived life that was seeking expression in him.

He never precisely defined what he meant by "image." But, in general, he meant a picture, likeness, or representation which was related to a psychic state. This image, either present in the environment or produced by the imagination, expressed deeper levels of the self he was coming to know.

He said that we meet ourselves in a thousand different dis-guises on the road of life. By paying attention to our images we can begin to understand more about who we are. We begin to live with an attitude which allows images to become symbolic for us. He stated that "every psychological expression is a sym-bol if we assume that it states or signifies something more and other than itself which eludes our present knowledge. This as-sumption is absolutely tenable wherever a consciousness exists which is attuned to the deeper meaning of things."[3] Consequent-ly, a fantasy figure, a sound, an aroma, a person, a place can all be images which are symbolic for us and lead us deeper into the mystery of our lives.

Jung located images in his dreams, his projections, and his feelings, and he engaged them in a process which he called "ac-tive imagination." We will discuss each one of these sources of images in turn. Jung's observations can be helpful in our own efforts to locate our symbols and be attuned to their meanings.

Dreams are the "royal road" to the unknown life within us, according to Freud. His *Interpretation of Dreams* was a pioneering, serious study of this phenomenon of human life. He saw meaning in the apparently jumbled images and stories of our sleeping hours.

Following the master, Jung worked with his own dreams and did extensive research on dreams in the course of his psychological work. His work brought him into contact with fifteen hundred to two thousand dreams a year. Without claiming to completely understand dreams and their role in our lives, he was able to draw some conclusions which are helpful in approaching dreams.

A fundamental premise is to have no preconceived meanings when dealing with dreams. "In fact," he writes, "it is always best to proceed as if the dream had no meaning at all, so as to be on one's guard against any possible bias."[4]

Dreams compensate for neglected areas of life. Jung believed that the psyche, through dreams, attempts to develop a balance, a harmony between the life that one is living and the neglected areas of personality which have not been owned. Dreams speak to us of our deeper selves. Diligent work with dreams, hopefully, can produce greater insight and broaden the horizons of personality.

Dreams point forward to potential wholeness as well as backward to unexamined causes. To say they are compensatory may oversimplify this complex phenomenon. Dreams appear to be able to "diagnose" a situation in life and predict future resolutions. They also look backward in retrospect at our sexual wishes and claims to power.

Amplification is a process used by Jung to explore the meaning of dreams. He broadened and enriched the dream imagery by making associations and using analogous images. I view the process of amplification as something similar to the effect of a pebble dropped into a pond and concentric circles spread out from the point of impact. If the pebble were a dream, then the circles spreading out from it are images and stories which amplify the dream.

For example, I may ask whether the dream has anything to do with events of the preceding day or immediate issues. Are there stories I may have read in novels, or may have seen on television or in the theater, which speak to me and perhaps relate to the dream imagery and enrich it? The circles used to amplify the dream may be as close as everyday life and extend all the way out to images and stories in mythology which give my dream context and direction.

Keeping a record of dreams is a helpful way of allowing the imagery to be present in our lives. One or two dreams may lead to little understanding. But in the course of time repetitions of patterns may emerge which may suggest meanings. Figures, events, the setting, and feelings should all be noted.

A rule of thumb is that each figure may relate to an aspect of our self, perhaps an ignored destructive aspect or a creative aspect seeking recognition. Another rule of thumb is that cluttered dreams may refer to my personal life, while simpler, more stark dreams may refer to the life of the times in which I am living. This collective meaning may be amplified by fairy tales and myths. The dreams should be looked at symbolically, that is, as having reference to inner psychic processes, but also concretely to see if they reveal an attitude I may have to events and people in daily life.

Working with dreams is obviously an intuitive realm. Some people have a wealth of dream imagery and learn a great deal from it. Other people look elsewhere for their imagery. Dreams are just not that available or significant for them. The point of attending to dreams, for those who can, is to develop communication with depths within me so that I may be more fully alive and integrated. My inner figures are strangers to me but they can become sources of insight, energy, and healing. Simply giving dreams room in my life by noting them and observing them is a good beginning.

A second source of imagery is the world around us which "catches" our projections. Projections are more universally available for attention than are dreams. By projection Jung meant that we unconsciously hurl unowned parts of self into the environment. We "project" on other people and they begin to represent ourselves without our knowing it.

Jung believed it was axiomatic that independent portions of the psyche become personified when given the chance for expression. He wrote: "Everything that works from the unconscious appears projected on others. Not that these others are wholly without blame, for even the worst projection is at least hung on a hook, perhaps a very small one, but still a hook offered by the other person."[5]

Possible "hooks" for our projections are personality features, mannerisms, appearance or other evident dimensions of someone else. Some people are simply more apt screens for certain projections than are other people. When the right hook or screen is available we project our fears, needs, desires and other aspects of our personality with which we are not acquainted. Our depths are using others to communicate with us.

People whom we admire can speak to us of ourselves. Rather than owning ourselves we are continually giving ourselves away through projections. Our admiration for the work and abilities of others may contain a hint that we too have similar or other abilities which we need to accept and develop. These images in our environment call us to our responsibilites. Of course, the people whom we intensely dislike may tell us something about ourselves, too, something we would rather not hear.

Our unacknowledged weaknesses are also projected. When we do not admit that we need healing or greater wisdom or learning or forgiving, we then tend to find these needs outside ourselves in others. We attribute these needs to them, not to ourselves. The Jungian analyst, Adolf Guggenbühl-Craig, writes about those people in helping professions who identify only with their helping role and do not admit a need to be helped themselves.[6] Regarding themselves only as helpers, they then have an inordinate need to find people who are looking for help, whether they be students, counselees, or sick people. The helper, through projection of her own weaknesses, keeps others in need of help and does not allow them to find their own source of healing or learning or health. If the projections were admitted and a helper could acknowledge these personal needs, then her helping could be even more beneficial. A healer who admits being wounded can allow wounded people to find their own healing powers.

While projections are inevitable, they eventually have to be withdrawn and owned if the contents are to be integrated into one's life. If we pay attention to the amount of emotion involved in a relationship we may be able to judge the extent of any projection taking place. Obviously projections are not the only basis for our relationships. Our likes and dislikes can be based on very real qualities in others. But extreme or inappropriate emotion can be a clue that projection is taking place. And this image which has caught our projection becomes a window to the self we are coming to know.

Along with dreams and projections, feelings are an important source of imagery. Jung believed that images were hidden in our feelings, so to speak, and the images could give us insight into the experiences causing the feelings. Feeling, affect, and mood can lead us to their source with the image as a vehicle.

In the period of his life when he was confronting his unconscious, Jung experimented with imaging his feelings. In that time of turmoil his feelings were particularly strong. He wrote:

> I was frequently so wrought up that I had to do certain yoga exercises in order to hold my emotions in check. But since it was my purpose to know what was going on within myself, I would do these exercises only until I had calmed myself enough to resume my work with the unconscious. As soon as I had the feeling that I was myself again, I abandoned this restraint upon the emotions and allowed the images and inner voices to speak afresh. . . .
>
> To the extent that I managed to translate the emotions into images—that is to say, to find the images which were concealed in the emotions—I was inwardly calmed and reassured. . . . As a result of my experiment, I learned how helpful it can be, from the therapeutic point of view, to find the particular images which lie behind emotions.[7]

One process that is frequently used to locate images in feelings is to allow images to bubble-up from within us onto an imaginary screen inside our head. Sitting quietly with our eyes closed, we can pay attention to the parade of images, looking for images that consistently appear and seem to express the feelings. This process allows the images to be unreflective and spontaneous.

Once we have the images to hold on to, we can then begin reflecting upon them so that we might grow in understanding and insight. The images lead us more profoundly into our experience and allow that experience to enter into the meaning of our lives. Our experience produces feelings; the feelings reveal images; the images lead to understanding and responsible living.

Jung worked with his inner images through a process which he called "active imagination." He noticed that when he played, both as a child and as an adult, he experienced a sense of peace and wholeness. In 1912, at the beginning of his difficult years, Jung took time each day after lunch to build a miniature village out of stones found by the lake. As a child this activity calmed him and so, he reasoned, it must be good for the soul. He played each day before his first patient arrived in the afternoon.

In this active imagination process Jung's energy was given form in the images of the village and he engaged the images in his play. Active imagination is principally a process of engaging one's images for a greater awareness of their meaning.

Through Jung's work the human imagination became a more respected and immensely helpful power. He said:

> The [imagination] is to be understood here as the real and literal power to create images—the classical use of the word in contrast to *phantasia,* which means a mere "conceit" in the sense of insubstantial thought. . . . [Imagination] is the active evocation of (inner) images . . . an authentic feat of thought or ideation, which does not spin aimless and groundless fantasies "into the blue"—does not, that is to say, just play with its objects, but tries to grasp the inner facts and portray them in images true to their nature.[8]

Jung's active imagination took many forms. He drew his images in journals. Drawing and painting the images made them vivid. He entered into dialogues with his inner figures to allow the voices expression in his life. He worked with stone, carving into it images and expressions of significance to him.

The forms of active imagination can be varied. Some people find it helpful to symbolize or image their experiences in the patterns of dance or in musical expression. Dreams can be returned to while awake and continued in a process of active imagination. It is possible to take scenes in a story, such as a Gospel story, and enter them imaginatively letting the scenes evolve into activity and dialogue which is not consciously structured.

This process has the potential for assisting a person's spiritual life. It is not that God is speaking to me directly through these images, even if they are religious images, but through the images I am led to depths where my God-given life is attempting to grow. If we think of ourselves as a word spoken by God, then in imaging and active imagination we are talking about ways of more clearly hearing the word we are.

In hearing the word and allowing it expression in our life, we are drawing closer to the God who speaks to us, who has given that life. In attending to these images our understanding is engaged and we then become responsible for what we now know. Our lives are affected as we attempt to respond to this awareness. This process is admirably demonstrated in the work of Teresa of Avila.

An Introduction to The Interior Castle

The Interior Castle of Teresa of Avila is a story. Teresa, the engaging story-teller, invites us into her life with God by stirring our imagination. The setting for her story is a castle which looms like a crystal globe. This crystal castle is entered by a "soul," the heroine or hero of the story, who begins a wonderful, at times harrowing, journey through the castle.

The outer environs of the castle are cold and dark. The land is crawling with snakes and other creatures. But as the soul enters the castle and begins to penetrate its inner recesses, the atmosphere gradually changes. The darkness gives way to light, a glow emanating from the center of the castle. The chilly air loses its edge and a warmth pervades the rooms comforting the guest. The story tells of the journey of the soul to the center of the castle where the King lives.

To reach the center of the castle the soul must roam through the many rooms of the castle. The rooms are arranged in seven concentric rings or circles around the center. But since the castle is actually global, the rings of rooms are like the leaves of a palm which enfold the center. Each ring, or dwelling place, consists of many rooms above, below, and to the side of one another. The dwelling place is a sheath of rooms around the center. The first dwelling place is all the rooms on the surface of the globe. Within that layer is the second dwelling place, the next sheath of rooms. In all, there are seven dwelling places which are milestones on the journey to the center, the seventh dwelling place actually being the center.

The images are fluid. The dwelling places contain rooms, but also gardens, fountains, and labyrinths. Each dwelling place is a world itself and unique experiences await the traveler. The center has a magnetic attraction which draws one through the dwelling places.

Teresa is telling us the story of her life of prayer. The journey through the castle is the story of a growing union with God as the soul enters more deeply into prayer. Prayer is the door to the castle and prayer is the activity which allows one to be drawn to God at the center. Teresa's relationship to God was alive within her and it grew through times of peace, tension, fulfillment, emptiness, and transition.

The first three dwelling places emphasize the efforts we humans make as we begin to enter a serious prayer relationship with God. Teresa characterizes these efforts as meditation or active prayer.

The first dwelling place speaks of the experience of one who is attempting to hear God's voice among the many voices in life. The person has begun to pray. An initial conversion has taken place. But the first rooms of the castle are closer to the outside than they are to the center. The outer darkness and the crawling things have invaded these rooms. In other words, an attentiveness to God at the center of one's life is difficult when so many things in life have themselves become "central." Having many centers causes the experience of the dark disorientation in the first rooms. Interestingly, the room that the soul is in is not dark itself, but it is experienced as dark because of the condition of the person entering it. In Teresa's words: "Even though it may not be in a bad state, it is so involved in worldly things and so absorbed with its possessions, honor, or business affairs, as I have said, that even though as a matter of fact it would want to see and enjoy its beauty these things do not allow it to; nor does it seem that it can slip free from so many impediments."[9] Because the individual is so fractured, it takes great effort to be attentive in prayer in the first dwelling place. But the journey has begun.

In the second dwelling place God's call is heard in a more personal way. The soul is gradually aware of being personally addressed and challenged. The person is entering a relationship with God and, as with other serious relationships, the involvement calls for more sensitive responses. Teresa writes that ". . . hearing His voice is a greater trial than not hearing it."[10]

The call from God to grow in a relationship with him reaches a person in a variety of ways. Teresa lists some of the ways: the words of good people, sermons, good books, illnesses, trials, moments in prayer. These occasions can speak to the heart and raise questions about oneself and life that call for a reorientation. More sharply hearing God's call will destabilize or decenter an individual and allow a true center to emerge. Teresa is emphatic on the purpose of prayer: "The whole aim of any person who is beginning prayer—and don't forget this, because it's very important—should be that he work and prepare himself with determination and every possible effort to bring his will into conformity with God's will."[11]

The third dwelling place is a time of settling down into a serious Christian life. Prayer is now an integral part of life and its effects are obvious in life's activities. In many ways, people characterized by the third dwelling place are models of an adult Christianity. "I believe that through the goodness of God there are many of these souls in the world," Teresa writes. "They long not to offend His Majesty, even guarding themselves against venial sins; they are fond of doing penance and setting aside periods for recollection; they spend their time well, practicing works of charity toward their neighbors, and are very balanced in their use of speech and dress and in the governing of their households—those who have them. Certainly, this is a state to be desired."[12] These people are living well-ordered lives, with enough energy left over to help others, to teach them how to achieve the same state.

However, alongside the apparent stability of the third dwelling place, another side of the picture begins to develop. Teresa uncovers signs which indicate that people in these rooms must prepare to move on. The journey of faith has to continue and the life of prayer must deepen and change. To overstay in the third dwelling place may lead to dangerous and difficult times. An anxiety may creep into these model lives. Prayer loses its vitality; a dryness sets in. Fears and too-tender sensitivities provoke a sense of losing control in life. These people try to do more of what they had been doing, in the belief that what had worked in the past will work now. But they cannot restore themselves to their former contentment. Teresa's diagnosis is that these apparently model Christians have not really abandoned themselves even though they live well-ordered lives. The signs indicate that they are being asked to let go of this stability, to move out of the third dwelling place and allow the King at the center to draw them ever deeper into the castle. Teresa says that they are being invited to enter into true contemplative prayer.

The fourth dwelling place marks a time of transition in the prayer life of the traveler. Prayer becomes less and less discursive or an activity totally controlled through human effort. Gradually, the experience becomes one of God drawing the soul into an interior state of recollection. The individual becomes passive in prayer. This infused prayer is the beginning of contemplation. And the fourth dwelling place is characterized by a degree of recollection which Teresa calls the prayer of quiet.

To distinguish between active meditation practiced in the

first three dwelling places and the contemplative prayer of quiet experienced in the fourth dwelling place, Teresa uses the example of two troughs of water. One is filled through great effort by means of long aqueducts. This activity is likened to active prayer. The other trough sits over a spring and fills quickly and easily. This trough is likened to contemplative prayer, which is begun in the fourth dwelling place.

Active prayer results in consolations (*contentos*) which are the result of human effort cooperating with God's grace. Contemplative prayer results in spiritual delights (*gustos*) which are passively received. The effects of such prayer in an individual are a lively faith, confidence, and freedom in the service of God.

The fifth dwelling place is a time of deepening contemplative prayer which Teresa calls the prayer of union. In this prayer there is an experience of union with God in which one "neither sees, nor hears, nor understands, because the union is always short and seems to the soul even much shorter than it probably is."[13] A sign that this brief union with God has taken place is the certitude of the soul that "it was in God and God was in it."[14] Teresa likens the experience to that of the silkworm that dies in the cocoon to be born a butterfly. The prayer of union is an experience of dying in Christ and rising to new life.

The sixth dwelling place represents an intensification of the union begun in the fourth dwelling place and heightened in the fifth dwelling place. In this lengthy section of *The Interior Castle*, Teresa relates the extraordinary mystical phenomena which she experienced. She refers to the experience as a betrothal and a time of purification in preparation for the spiritual marriage of the last dwelling place. It is a night of the spirit with interior and exterior trials.

The experience of God in this prayer is like a fire in the heart. She writes: "I do know that it seems this pain reaches to the soul's very depths and that when He who wounds it draws out the arrow, it indeed seems in accord with the deep love the soul feels that God is drawing these very depths after Him."[15] This union with God results in powerful imaginative, intellectual, and physical effects which require courageous living. "The best remedy . . . is to engage in external works of charity and to hope in the mercy of God, who never fails those who hope in Him."[16] The pain and joy in this sixth dwelling place are equally intense. The raptures of this betrothal are compared to the tumult experienced by St. Paul when he was hurled to the ground on his way to Damascus.

In the seventh dwelling place the union with God is completed. Teresa reports an intellectual vision of the Trinity and a perduring awareness of the Trinity's presence. An imaginative vision of Christ introduces the experience of union which she terms the spiritual marriage, the culmination of the journey through the castle. This experience of union is at a deep interior level which Teresa calls the spirit. "One can say no more—insofar as can be understood—than that the soul, I mean the spirit, is made one with God."[17]

The union is as total as rain falling into a river. This life in Christ is judged in time by its effects. The disturbances of the sixth dwelling place disappear. A deep interior peace is a constant state. And, finally, the journey into the castle propels one back into the world: "This is the reason for prayer, my daughters, the purpose of this spiritual marriage: the birth always of good works, good works."[18]

Reading The Interior Castle Through Its Images

A striking feature of *The Interior Castle* is its imagery. Beginning with the castle itself, Teresa's story is a network of images engaging the reader in a world of shape and color and feeling. Teresa is driven to imaginative descriptions because her experiences are too subtle to be captured simply in concepts. While she will often report that her experiences are beyond understanding, she will still offer the reader a metaphor or simile in order to begin to convey the meaning of her experience.

Teresa has been called a psychological mystic. While her prayer experiences frequently are inexpressible and confound understanding, she nevertheless attempts a psychological description of the effects of these experiences in her. The journey to God in the castle, she makes clear, is also a journey to self, to the fullness of one's life. These two goals are concomitant aspects of the same journey. Movement toward one goal affects movement toward the other goal.

Union with God, as Teresa unfolds her story, may have its ineffable, inexpressible dimension, but the movement toward the deepest self certainly has expressible effects on the human psyche. Teresa is using prose and poetic imagery to communicate to us the effects in her psyche of a growing union with God.

The images she uses do not appear to be mere pedagogical devices, or just another way of saying what she means. Teresa's imagery appears to be more closely connected to her experience than such didactic images would be. She is related to many of these images at a level deeper than conscious choice. Some of them have a long history in her life. Rather than translating her thought into images, she gives the impression of one who is thinking in images, and these images are natural expressions of her experiences.

The very inconsistency of her imagery, the fading of one image and the appearance of another, is evidence of the presence of symbol. Edward Edinger's comment concerning dream imagery is pertinent: "Whenever we encounter in dreams an image which undergoes such numerous transformations, we can be sure we are dealing with a particularly potent and dynamic symbol."[19]

Teresa's images are pregnant with meaning, and that is the condition of a living symbol. A living symbol itself conveys meaning to the observer and does not rely solely on the meaning given it by the author. Furthermore, it is possible that the meaning of the symbol is not to be located entirely in the original experience of Teresa. Carl Jung's theories of the human psyche hypothesize a collective or transpersonal level which contains patterns of meaning. Teresa's images may have meaning in themselves which is the result of realities and conditions that are prior to her personal experience. In fact these symbols may shape her experience and at the same time convey its meaning.

Our exploration of the images in *The Interior Castle* will assume this transpersonal level of psyche which offers patterns of meaning.

While we are studying the images from the point of view of depth psychology, Jung's theories will be more comprehensively treated. This work is meant to be a study of Teresa of Avila's spirituality, but it is also meant to be an introduction to the psychology of C. G. Jung. Not all aspects of Jung's theories are immediately relevant to *The Interior Castle* imagery, but I believe that there is benefit in placing Teresa's teachings and Jung's theories side-by-side for the creative comparisons of the reader. Because Jung's work is extensive and relatively new, a good portion of this study will be devoted to a presentation of his psychology.

Carl Jung's theories are by no means unchallenged today. Aspects of his theories, such as the reality of the collective unconscious and the existence of archetypes, are frequently questioned. This study will assume the adequacy of his theories, and not defend them. His theories are a way of saying that the human personality acts "as if" such-and-such were so. As an interpretation of experiences of human interiority, I find Jung's psychology extremely helpful. For the purpose of this study, he offers us the opportunity to examine a classic document in the mystical tradition through a contemporary interpretive framework. It is encouraging to know that this framework has been beneficial for great numbers of people.

To the extent that Teresa's imagery is related to a collective layer of the psyche, it is then a guide to meanings that are not the sole possession of a sixteenth century, Spanish, cloistered nun but belong to the human psyche across time and culture. Her story can become our story and her symbols can lead us into our own depths where God waits.

In addition, exploration of her images can help us find our own images. With these personal symbols we can begin to tell our particular myth, our symbols-in-narrative, as Teresa has done in *The Interior Castle*. And as we tell that story we stand forth in the life given us by God, and we become our self-for-God.

The specific images we will be studying in *The Interior Castle* are these: castle, water, journey, serpent and devil, butterfly, marriage, and Christ. I have chosen these images primarily for two reasons. In the first place, these images are obvious and major symbols in the work and they greatly carry the story. They, however, do not exhaust Teresa's imagery. Secondly, Jungian theory has something to say about these particular images, or images quite similar to them. These two criteria, certainly subjective in part, led naturally to the list of images we will be studying.

Briefly, the castle image calls us to center our lives. Water speaks to the hidden depths which contain a great deal of our life. Journey as an image alerts us to passages or transitions which will inevitably be part of our development. Serpents and devils express the darkness we experience in life, and butterflies remind us of the newness that comes to be in the darkness. Marriage expresses the healing and wholeness we ache for, within our persons, within our communities, and with God. And finally, the symbol of Christ points to the fullness of life we attain when we are in union with the divine presence in our lives.

Images and Religious Experience

In reflecting upon *The Interior Castle*, I believe it is possible to say that Teresa was using a process of active imagination. She was taking the images which spoke to her of her experiences with God and engaging them in a literary form. As one might sculpt or paint images, Teresa imbedded hers in a story for reading and reflection. The story expresses her religious experience. Teresa is communicating her transformations, her conversions, through image.

Jung writes about the role of image in human experience. It is important to note that image aids our spirituality when we enter into our experience with the belief that God is calling us to union. Teresa's entire castle story is the result of hearing God in her life.

The call to conversion is a disconcerting experience generally. And it is in the consternation of such a call that image finds

its role. An author who has emphasized this role of image in religious experience is an Episcopal priest, Urban Holmes. In
Ministry and Imagination Holmes maintains that imagination is
critical in hearing God's word in life. By imagination he is referring to the intuitive, feeling dimensions of experience which express themselves in image. Ministers who have developed this
imaginative ability are better able to help others on their religious journeys.

Conversion requires that we hear God in a new way in our
life and the experience is often preceded by crisis. Holmes describes the situation using categories developed by Victor
Turner, a social anthropologist, who speaks of structures, anti-
structures, and liminal experiences.[20]

Structure, as I understand Holmes' discussion, is a way of
describing my situation when I am living an orderly existence.
My life is under control and I can well articulate who I am and
where I am going. The anti-structure is a way of describing my
situation when my former cosmos becomes chaos. In other
words, the certainties of my life are gone and my normal understandings are not operative. Liminal experiences are those transition experiences I have as I move between the structure and
the anti-structure, and back to structure again.

If we apply these terms to *The Interior Castle* we could say
that the movement into the castle from the outer environs is a
movement from structure into the anti-structure. And the experiences within the castle are liminal experiences, experiences of
passage.

Holmes stresses the importance of image in the anti-structure. Image is the only language left. Experiences which are calling me to conversion have subverted my world and I have been
carried out into the wilderness. My experience is obviously
powerful and potentially rich; my feelings are abundant. But
my words cannot as yet carry the weight of the new meanings
being born in the darkness of the anti-structure.

In these times the image can be a vehicle for carrying the
feelings and the meanings which I cannot articulate. Images
help me to hold on to the experience, stay with it, and communicate it. The communication is not only to others but to myself as

well. I am listening for God's voice in the situation, listening with fewer filters in the darkness of the anti-structure than I would have in the sunlight of structure.

Gradually, I will have words to go with my images. The symbol gives rise to thought. The image and the concept begin to capture the fullness of the experience. The image has helped capture the intuitive, feeling side of the experience and given the experience some manageable form. The concepts begin to capture the understandings resulting from the experience and help to define again my world and what I now need to do and be. I am back in the structure again. It has been an experience of dying and rising. The Christian symbols extend and contextualize my personal images.

In the above discussion I have used Urban Holmes as a source for two reasons. In the first place, Holmes' writing is quite compatible with Jung's understanding of the role of image. As a matter of fact, Jung is a source for Holmes. Their compatibility will become clearer when we discuss the symbol-formation process of the psyche in a later chapter. Secondly, Holmes extends the implications of the psychological theory into the realms of religious experience and speaks of God communicating with us in the experience of darkness and confusion.

The Interior Castle, as a document of religious experience, is describing a series of conversions or transformations. The call of God moved Teresa into the unknown, into the anti-structure with its liminal experiences. The images in her document can be understood as symbolic vehicles for the greater awareness and new meanings born in the unknown. We will explore these images in the following chapters in an attempt to better understand the relationship between Teresa's call from God and her psychological development, her emerging personhood. The first image to be discussed is the image of the castle.

Concluding Reflections and Suggestions

In the beginning of this chapter I referred to Teresa of Avila as a story-teller. The process she engaged in, which resulted in *The Interior Castle,* was a process of writing her own story, her images-in-narrative. Jung's psychology stressed the centrality of image in human experience. Together they suggest that I approach my life as a story.

Transforming experiences which invite conversion abruptly halt my story. The images which arise in the new situation become elements of a renewed story. Jung has located certain sources for these images. By allowing these images to speak to me the narrative of my life begins again. I can find a story line and continue to tell my story.

And I must tell the story if it is to become my story. In the telling of my experiences through the images and words related to those experiences I begin to own the experiences and allow them to shape me. In telling my story I appropriate the person I am becoming as a result of that story.

In other words, religious experience is not religious experience until it is communicated. I communicate it when I find some way of paying attention to, and reflecting upon, the experience. The communication may only be from myself to myself, but I am attending to my experience when I story it and I am hearing that experience as it is storied.

The experience of the disciples on the road to Emmaus is an example of people storying their experience. These disciples had listened to Jesus' parables. The purpose of at least some of Jesus' stories was to cause a "dark interval," an evocative term suggested by John Crossan.[21] Jesus was attempting through his stories to subvert the world view of his listeners so that they would be open to hearing the news of the kingdom. The unexpected events in the parables jarred the expectations of the audience. In effect, the parable became a liminal experience moving the listeners into the anti-structure.

Still, the disciples who had heard the parables had not deeply experienced this dark interval. It was only when Jesus the parabler became Jesus the parable that they found themselves subverted. When the outcome of Jesus' life confused them, and not just the outcome of his stories, they could only say from the despair of their darkness: "We were hoping that he was the one who would set Israel free" (Lk. 24:21).

In that apparently hopeless situation Jesus encouraged the

travelers to Emmaus to begin to tell their story. "What are you discussing as you go your way?" And they began to report the events of the past few days and they told of their confusion.

After hearing their story, Jesus told the story of the Jewish people as recorded in their Scriptures. He showed them that the Scriptures help provide meaning for their recent experiences. The conjunction of the disciples' story with God's story in Scripture allowed the disciples to recognize the Lord in their midst.

The material in this chapter suggests that storying happens not only through the recounting of events but through careful attention to non-reflective, spontaneous imagery that communicates depth experiences. This imagery, rooted in a level below conscious grasp, helps to turn the events of the days into meaningful invitations to enter life more fully and there recognize the Lord.

The power of images has impressed me on numerous occasions. One time, while directing a retreat, I asked the group to take time and reflect on areas of their lives which seemed to call for attention. I suggested that they find some symbolic expression for these areas in the hope that the symbol might help them find meaning and movement in their life. And I offered them an opportunity to share these symbolic expressions with the group as a way of aiding their own listening to the story they were telling. Many in the group wished to share, while the others felt free to be supportive through careful listening.

One man wrote a poem. His metaphors, drawn from nature, showed him struggling with his vulnerability. Reading the poem was an emotional effort. Another man, whose avocation was music, simply made a statement couched in terms of music. He said he had a desire for someone else to write the song of his life. He had been living his own songs but now was willing to let someone else write the music for his life. His image was a revealing expression of a willingness to "let go," to decenter himself and let God emerge as his center. These meanings were not so explicitly stated, but we could hear and feel that something like that was beginning to take shape in him. Images are powerful containers for emotions, and the emotional difficulty these men had in expressing themselves demonstrated that the images were reaching deep into their experience.

One of the women sang a song she had written during the reflection time. Another showed three rather abstract pastel drawings without offering any comment. A third woman, speaking from a precarious situation in her life, actually enacted a well-known fairytale for us, showing that its story was her story. She commented that the outcome of the fairytale challenged her to remain faithful to commitments in her life.

A man in the group drew a time-line showing the peaks, valleys, and plateaus of his life as they corresponded to his age. His comments filled-in the lines and numbers which movingly drew him into his story.

Not all of the people on retreat were comfortable "imaging" their lives. And not all who did find symbols were comfortable sharing them. I believe that it was important to have everyone at least consider the presence and action of symbols in life. If Jung is correct, our lives are addressing us through such symbolic expression. And we need not be songwriters or poets to find images. They are all around us in people and places; they fill our memories. And when we look at our religion we realize that the images and dogmas of Christianity are symbolic expressions of the experience of mystery which is at the core of life.

While some of the people on retreat spoke of the joy and gratitude they felt for God's presence in their lives, the majority appeared to have a need to symbolize the "dark intervals" they were experiencing. They listened to God, through images, while in the anti-structure.

In this setting, the experiences which they related were not named "failure" or "mistake." They were seen as the ways in which individual lives uniquely enter the paschal mystery. Our faith helped us to discover renewed life in the darkness. We read the words of Jesus at the Last Supper, and we shared bread together.

Our stories did not end with this retreat, nor were all problems solved or wounds healed. This experience of symbolizing did not provide an answer to life. But the effort was effective in helping us to hear more clearly the story we are living with

God. We listened to our story in the belief that our most basic story is the Jesus story with all its power and hope.

NOTES

1. C.G. Jung, *Memories, Dreams, Reflections,* ed. Aniela Jaffe (New York: Random House, Vintage Books, 1965).

2. Ibid., p. 199.

3. C.G. Jung, *Collected Works* (Princeton University Press), VI, 817. In citing references to the *Collected Works* the first number is the volume, the second number is the paragraph.

4. Ibid., XVII, 263.

5. Ibid., VIII, 99.

6. Adolf Guggenbühl-Craig, *Power in the Helping Professions* (Zurich: Spring Publications, 1971), pp. 89ff.

7. Jung, *Memories,* p. 177.

8. Jung, C.W., XII, 219.

9. Teresa of Avila, *The Interior Castle,* trans. Kieran Kavanaugh and Otilio Rodriguez (New York: Paulist Press, 1979), I, chap. 2, no. 14.

10. Ibid., II, chap. 1, no. 2.

11. Ibid., II, chap. 1, no.8.

12. Ibid., III, chap. 1, no. 5.

13. Ibid., V, chap. 1, no. 8.

14. Ibid., V, chap. 1, no. 8.

15. Ibid., VI, chap. 2, no. 4.

16. Ibid., VI, chap. 1, no. 13.

17. Ibid., VII, chap. 2, no. 3.

18. Ibid., VII, chap. 4, no. 6.

19. Edward Edinger, *Ego and Archetype* (Baltimore: Penguin Books, Inc., 1973), p. 121.

20. Urban T. Holmes III, *Ministry and Imagination* (New York: Seabury Press, 1976), pp. 119–123.

21. John Dominic Crossan, *The Dark Interval* (Niles, Ill.: Argus Communications, 1975).

CHAPTER TWO

The Castle, An Image of Wholeness

Often in our lives we become aware of predominant images which speak to us of wholeness. Certain images, whether a particular person, or a specific place, or a piece of music, or a picture, powerfully affect us. They seem to speak to the core of who we are or hope to be. They help to center us and give focus to our lives. To pay attention to them is like coming home.

This chapter explores one such type of image, the mandala symbol, and it presents Teresa's symbolic expression of wholeness, the castle.

Mandala Symbolism

Carl Jung noted the tendency of the human psyche to use a sphere or circle to express fullness or wholeness. These psychic images he called "mandalas," a sanskrit word meaning circle. He wrote of the mandala: "In the sphere of religious practices and in psychology it denotes circular images, which are drawn, painted, modelled, or danced. Plastic structures of this kind are to be found, for instance, in Tibetan Buddhism, and as dance figures these circular patterns occur also in Dervish monasteries. As psychological phenomena they appear spontaneously in dreams, in certain states of conflict, and in cases of schizophrenia. Very frequently they contain a quaternity or a multiple of four, in the form of a cross, a star, a square, an octagon, etc."[1]

In another place he lists some of the formal elements of mandalas. They are circular, spherical or egg-shaped in form. A center is imaged as a sun, star, or cross. And frequently the mandala is presented in the motif of city, courtyard, or castle.[2]

In 1918–1919 Jung sketched a circular drawing in his notebook every morning. These mandalas gave him insight into the development of his personality, a sense of the meanings growing in him. "My mandalas," he wrote, "were cryptograms concerning the state of the self which were presented to me anew each day. In them I saw the self—that is, my whole being—actively at work."[3]

The mandala as a symbol of the self is the psyche's expression of its fundamental orientation to wholeness. Not only is it an expression of the goal, but it also indicates that the psyche has a built-in dynamism moving it toward its objective. In cases of conflict the psyche often spontaneously produces a mandala as an indication of the possibility of a resolution. Jung studied the mandalas drawn by his patients in the process of active imagination. A number of the mandalas have been included in his *Collected Works*.[4]

The reality of such an imaging process in the psyche was confirmed for me when I had an opportunity to observe the work of an impressive Jungian analyst, Mrs. Dora Kalff. Mrs. Kalff was encouraged by Carl Jung to become an analyst after he noted her intuitive ability with children. In time she became a pioneer in the treatment of disturbed children, and mandala forms became an integral aspect of the treatment.

As Mrs. Kalff explained it, the child must internalize a healthy sense of self in the first year or two of life. When the child has experienced security through the mother, the totality expressed in the mother-child unity begins to take root within the child. A sense of self is born.

After approximately a year the totality within the child seeks an outside expression in the child's play. The type of play and the patterns formed with play materials demonstrates that the child has experienced the totality of the self away from the mother.

Children who, through poor "bonding" with the mother,

have not developed an inward totality demonstrate a lack of harmony and wholeness in their play images. For such children, Mrs. Kalff's treatment provides an effective means of establishing the missing sense of self.

In Mrs. Kalff's studio outside of Zurich there are trays of sand in which the children play. The trays are just large enough to fill the peripheral vision of the child so that this world of play can be viewed as one whole scene. The child may choose play figures from among literally hundreds available on shelves in the studio. The shelves are stocked with human figures, animals, religious symbols, dwellings, and so forth.

There are no rules. The child is free to build anything or to play in any way within the confines of the sand tray. The tray becomes a free, protected space for the expression of the child. It is, in effect, a mandala giving bounds to the child's developing psyche. Where the mother-child relationship has not allowed the child to interiorize the totality of self, the sand tray becomes a feminine, secure place nourishing tentative self-images in play.

In the beginning of the child's play, the boundaries of the sand tray and the watchfulness of Mrs. Kalff help establish limits so that the child will not hurt himself. The offering of a free, protected space is a recognition of the healing function of the psyche.

In time, a transformation of energy will occur and destructive activity will give way to constructive play. This turning point is usually an automatic happening. Occasionally, Mrs. Kalff gives direction when she intuitively knows that the moment has arrived.

The signs that an inner sense of self is being established are found in the images of play. For example, Mrs. Kalff interpreted the appearance of messengers bearing secrets and caves filled with precious stones as indications of a child's inner centering. Play figures begin to balance one another in their characteristics, for example masculine and feminine, and the play takes on a harmony previously missing. Dwellings may appear on hilltops, further testifying to the centering process. Mandala images are appearing within the mandala of the sand tray.

With this experience of the totality of the self, the child's energies are freed and a positive relationship with the outer world is initiated. An ego identity can now be built on the base of the self. The father is an important figure in this ego development.

Teresa's Castle As A Mandala Symbol

Teresa of Avila's image of the castle gives every indication of being a mandala symbol. The very title of Teresa's work introduces us to the image of the castle. The castle becomes the site of the soul's experiences. It is an image that encompasses the entire story, from the beginning in the outer courtyard to the conclusion in the center. Within this image other images unfold as a theater within a theater. The other images will often stray from the castle theme, but then its dwelling places will return as a basic orientation.

Teresa's use of the castle reminds one of a net that hauls up a variety of sea life from deep waters. The sea life threatens to spill out but the net holds. Similarly, the castle image is pushed and shoved by the lively images within, but it does hold its shape.

Teresa's castle is actually different in structure from what we would assume. A careful reading of her description reveals unique characteristics. In the beginning of *The Interior Castle* she writes: "Today while beseeching our Lord to speak for me because I wasn't able to think of anything to say nor did I know how to begin to carry out this obedience, there came to my mind what I shall now speak about, that which will provide us with a basis to begin with. It is that we consider our soul to be like a castle made entirely out of a diamond or of very clear crystal, in which there are many rooms, just as in heaven there are many dwelling places."[5]

Fr. Diego de Yepes, an early biographer of Teresa, adds further description. He maintains that two or three years after writing *The Interior Castle* Teresa told him that the idea of using a castle as her chief image came in an instant. She was able to envision "a most beautiful crystal globe like a castle in which she saw seven dwelling places, and in the seventh, which was in the center, the King of Glory dwelt in the greatest splendor. From there He beautified and illumined all those dwelling places to the outer wall. The inhabitants received more light the nearer they were to the center. Outside of the castle all was darkness, with toads, vipers, and other poisonous vermin."[6]

The exact nature of this creative moment remains unknown. At the very least it could be said that Teresa's imagination produced a highly original image in a spontaneous manner. The castle does not appear to be a conscious construct as much as it seems to be an unreflective occurrence which results in Teresa discovering the image already present.

The spontaneous and compelling nature of the event indicates an autonomous activity of her psyche. The psyche spoke in its own language of imagery and produced the symbol of the castle as a crystal globe. Even if Teresa's choice of the castle as her primary image were more conscious and deliberate than is indicated, she is still employing an image of universal appeal and immense psychic power. The castle is recognizable as a mandala figure.

The mandalas of Dora Kalff's sand tray and Teresa's castle display striking similarities. Obviously the sand tray is a physical space and the image is developed through concrete objects. Through these materials the psyche is expressing itself in an outward manner. The castle of Teresa is a literary construction which suggests to the reader a place of the imagination. The psyche is invited to express itself in an inner theater.

Just as Dora Kalff offers a free, protected space to the child, Teresa invites the adult to freely wander among the images she provides, and their own inner images as well. "Considering the strict enclosure," she writes, "and the few things you have for your entertainment, my Sisters, and that your buildings are not always as large as would be fitting for your monasteries, I think it will be a consolation for you to delight in this interior castle since without permission from the prioress you can enter and take a walk through it at any time."[7] She is encouraging an exercise in active imagination, a time of play as important to the adult as to the child.

In the protected space of the sand tray the child is attempting to experience an inner totality for the first time. In the space of the castle the adult is attempting to reconstellate the totality which has been lost as the ego emerges.

In a later discussion of Jung's psychology the relationship between the ego and self will be described more carefully. For now it is important to know that the two are not identical, and that the ego in its development loses contact with the ground of its more complete life, the self.

As the traveler through the castle approaches God at the center, the self is reconstellated and the ego is once again related to it. Teresa has her own language for the necessity of this relationship:

> It seems I'm saying something foolish. For if this castle is the soul, clearly one doesn't have to enter it since it is within oneself. How foolish it would seem were we to tell someone to enter a room he is already in. But you must understand that there is a great difference in the ways one may be inside the castle. For there are many souls who are in the outer courtyard—which is where the guards stay—and don't care at all about entering the castle, nor do they know what lies within that most precious place, nor who is within, nor even how many rooms it has. You have already heard in some books on prayer that the soul is advised to enter within itself; well that's the very thing I'm advising.[8]

A Pilgrimage to the Center

The mandala focuses attention on the center. The circle allows a center to emerge and the center then organizes the chaos about it. Patterns of meaning develop in relationship to the center. This section will elaborate on the notion of the center and view the journey through the castle as a pilgrimage to the center. Pilgrimage proves to be a helpful concept in elaborating Teresa's journey motif.

Carl Jung became convinced of the importance of the center to psychological development. The center represents the self, the goal of development. Human development consists in circumambulation of the self.

The fact that everything points to the center was confirmed for Jung in a dream he had shortly after his years of troubled searching. He related the dream in his autobiography:

> I found myself in a dirty, sooty city. It was night, and winter, dark, and raining. I was in Liverpool. With a number of Swiss—say, half a dozen—I walked through the dark streets. I had the feeling that there we were coming from the harbor, and that the real city was actually up above, on the cliffs. We climbed up there. It reminded me of Basel, where the market is down below and then you go up through the Totengässchen ("Alley of the Dead"), which leads to a plateau above and so to the Petersplatz and the Peterskirche. When we reached the plateau, we found a broad square dimly illuminated by street lights, into which many streets converged. The various quarters of the city were arranged radially around the square. In the center was a round pool, and in the middle of it a small island. While everything round about was obscured by rain, fog, smoke and dimly lit darkness, the little island blazed with sunlight. On it stood a single tree, a magnolia, in a shower of reddish blossoms. It was as though the tree stood in the sunlight and were at the same time the source of light.[9]

Jung said that this dream brought him a sense of finality: "I saw that here the goal had been revealed. One could not go beyond the center. The center is the goal, and everything is directed toward that center. Through this dream I understood that the self is the principle and archetype of orientation and meaning. Therein lies its healing function. For me, this insight signified an approach to the center and therefore to the goal. Out of it emerged a first inkling of my personal myth."[10]

The similarity between Teresa's intuitive vision of the crystal castle and Jung's dream is evident. Both mandala images accentuate a center which draws all else. The center is a source of light, a means of orientation. It is a goal of a journey.

In *The Interior Castle* the individual gradually moves toward the center, passing from one dwelling place to another. This procession through the castle has characteristics of a pilgrimage and it is useful to illumine the journey through that concept. The individual is a pilgrim who is journeying to a place where the human and divine meet.

The relationship between the mystical way and a pilgrimage has been highlighted by Victor and Edith Turner in *Image and Pilgrimage in Christian Culture*. They state: "... pilgrimage may be thought of as extroverted mysticism, just as mysticism is introverted pilgrimage. The pilgrim physically traverses a mystical way; the mystic sets forth on an interior spiritual pilgrimage. For the former, concreteness and historicity dominate; for the latter, a phased interior process leads to a goal beyond conceptualization."[11]

A comparison of the characteristics of a pilgrimage with the characteristics of Teresa's journey through the castle demonstrates the similarities of the two ventures.

The basic paradigm for every Christian pilgrimage is the way of the cross. That journey is the pre-eminent journey to the center. Each shrine has its unique images and characteristics but each is also a sacred space partaking of the center. Whether the journey is across the sea to the Holy Land or simply a short ride to a local shrine, the same journey is being taken when one is on pilgrimage.

Each shrine has a predominant symbol which mediates the entire pilgrimage. The dominant symbol gives unity and flow to the journey. There are also other images, sub-symbols, which are connected with the main symbol by association. These symbols form a type of system through which the traveler must pass in order to approach the center. Often the pilgrim is not allowed to approach the center directly, but must circle it before entering the shrine.

The Marian shrine in Einsiedeln, Switzerland, was an experience for me of the still-powerful activity of pilgrimage. The Benedictine Abbey in Einsiedeln, founded by St. Meinrad, contains in its church a shrine of the Black Madonna. Devotion to this Madonna is particularly strong among Germanic peoples.

The sense impressions within the church tumble upon one another. The height and depth of its sacred space provide an atmosphere for attentive listening. The obvious age of the structure abolishes normal time-frames. The press of time eases and a feeling of timelessness takes over.

At the back of the church, where one enters, stands the shrine, a chapel containing the image of the Black Madonna. The chapel is surrounded by banks of flickering candlelight, providing a glow within the dark interior of the church. Inside the chapel the colors are brilliant: the deep black of the Madonna's face, the glistening gold of her clothing and surrounding ornamentation, and the bright colors of flowers.

It is a true center, the focal point of the many images of sight and sound associated with it. The organ music, the chant of the monks, and the litanies of the people blend with all other sense impressions to evoke a place of numinosity. The power of the shrine opens the pilgrim to the mystery of existence where the divine and human meet.

The power of pilgrimage is such because the pilgrim has left her normal world and entered another realm. In Victor Turner's categories, the pilgrimage is a quasi-liminal experience in which the individual voluntarily moves out of structure into anti-structure. It is quasi-liminal because the movement is voluntary. The pilgrim allows the dislocation.

In the anti-structure of the pilgrimage, one's daily routines and relationships are absent. A community of travelers flows past boundaries, even national ones. Wayside chapels overlook the route, heightening the expectation, and aiding the decompression which allows the pilgrims freedom from their normal preoccupations. The stages of the journey allow the pilgrim to be more and more attentive to the center and the call of God in life.

As a journey through the anti-structure to the center, the

pilgrimage physically moves through regions of image. The language of pilgrimage is symbol and myth. The pilgrimage becomes a free, protected space-in-motion where pilgrims playfully engage the symbols and open themselves to transformation. It is a contemplative activity. And it is a prayer of the feet.

Fundamental to all pilgrimage, however, is the interior footwork. The interior footwork is the pilgrimage that Teresa of Avila is advocating when she invites her sisters, and the reader, to travel through the seven dwelling places, reminding us that "in each of these there are many others, below and above and to the sides, with lovely gardens and fountains and labyrinths, such delightful things that you would want to be dissolved in praises of the great God who created the soul in His own image and likeness."[12]

Just as the Madonna is the dominant symbol of Einsiedeln, the castle, for Teresa, is the primary and uniting image. The other images are related to it as sub-symbols, some more closely related to the castle theme than others. But all are wayside chapels marking a labyrinthine way to the center.

Teresa has created an internal anti-structure, a free space away from the enclosures of the body and mind. Her invitation is to a pilgrimage. Her language is the symbolic language of pilgrimage. She invites a wandering, a playing among the images.

In this free and protected space it is possible to hear more and more clearly the call of the center. Along with the symbols she proposes, Teresa leaves room for the personal symbols of the reader which may begin to populate the route to the shrine. Attention to these images puts the true pilgrim in touch with levels of life where God heals and calls to union. God is met and the self is born on this journey.

As G.K. Chesterton explained, the purpose of all journey is to come home. Each image shares the center and each image slowly reveals the center to us as we find ourselves becoming centered. Jung wrote: "The man whose sun still moves round the earth is essentially different from the man whose earth is a satellite of the sun."[13]

The Tower: Jung's Pilgrimage in Stone

Although Teresa and Carl Jung were primarily engaged in a timeless inner world, they could not neglect the outer world of time and space. Just as the external pilgrimage required an inner journey at the same time, the inner pilgrimage made demands on the outer environment. Both Teresa and Jung built "castles" of wood and stone to mirror their inner structures.

In Teresa's case, the convents she established in her reform movement became the mandala forms symbolizing her inner pilgrimage to God. Her work in establishing these new communities is the topic of the next section.

Jung's outer imaging of his inner life took the shape of a structure he called the "Tower." It was his attempt to live a symbolic life, something he felt was desperately needed in our contemporary situation:

> You see, man is in need of a symbolic life—badly in need. We only live banal, ordinary, rational, or irrational things—which are naturally also within the scope of rationalism, otherwise, you could not call them irrational. But we have no symbolic life. Where do we live symbolically? Nowhere, except where we participate in the ritual of life. But who, among the many, are really participating in the ritual of life? Very few. . . .
>
> Have you got a corner somewhere in your house where you perform the rites, as you can see in India? Even the very simple houses there have at least a curtained corner where the members of the household can lead the symbolic life, where they can make their new vows or meditation. We don't have it; we have no such corner. We have our own rooms, of course—but there is a telephone which can ring us up at any time, and we always must be ready. We have no time, no place. . . .
>
> Now we have no symbolic life, and we are all badly in need of the symbolic life. Only the symbolic life can express the need of the soul—the daily need of the soul, mind you! And because people have no such

thing, they can never step out of this mill—this awful, grinding, banal life in which they are "nothing but.". . .

These things go pretty deep, and no wonder people get neurotic. Life is too rational; there is no symbolic existence in which I am fulfilling my role, my role as one of the actors in the divine drama of life.[14]

Jung became specific and concrete about his symbolic life. He built a retreat for himself away from the city of Kusnacht on the upper Lake of Zurich. "Gradually, through my scientific work," he wrote, "I was able to put my fantasies and the contents of the unconscious on a solid footing. Words and paper, however, did not seem real enough to me; something more was needed. I had to achieve a kind of representation in stone of my innermost thoughts and of the knowledge I had acquired. Or, to put it another way, I had to make a confession of faith in stone. That was the beginning of the 'Tower,' the house which I built for myself at Bollingen."[15]

At first he intended to build a one-story hut similar to huts he had seen in Africa with the fire in the center spot. But that plan proved too primitive, so the Tower was built with two stories. In this place he could be renewed and peaceful. There was no telephone, no electricity. It was simple and circular, a timeless place where his ancestors would have felt at home. The waters of the lake lapped at its foundations.

In four years he built again. This time an annex contained a private meditation room where his number two personality painted on the walls and felt outside time and space. "Thus the second tower became for me a place of spiritual concentration."[16]

In the course of twelve years four different parts of the Tower were constructed. For Jung it was a mandala-like expression of the whole personality which he had engaged in his work and meditations. The Tower was an image in stone of his journey into the psyche.

Living in the Tower, Jung lived a symbolic life. It put him in touch with life at deep levels: "At times I feel as if I am spread out over the landscape and inside things, and am myself living in every tree, in the splashing of the waves, in the clouds and the animals that come and go, in the procession of the seasons. There is nothing in the Tower that has not grown into its own form over the decades, nothing with which I am not linked. Here everything has its history, and mine; here is space for the spaceless kingdom of the world's and the psyche's hinterland."[17]

The Tower represented a strong association with the feminine. Jung began building the first part two months after the death of his mother. "It represented for me the maternal hearth."[18] In the year of his wife's death he added an upper portion to represent his ego-personality, the extension of consciousness he had achieved in old age.

Jung's Tower at Bollingen was in the vicinity of Einsiedeln and the shrine of the Black Madonna in St. Meinrad's Abbey. I visited the Tower while traveling with a group of people who were going to the Marian shrine.

The Tower is in a clump of trees and bushes by the lake and located many yards from the road. Because members of the Jung family still use the building we were prepared for a long-distance glimpse of the place. But we were noticed by the family and one of the members invited us into the courtyard for a closer view.

We saw paintings by Jung on the roof over an outdoor fireplace in which the evening meal was being cooked. The paintings were of family emblems of heraldry. To the left of the hearth was a stone inscription Jung had chiseled on the occasion of his wife's death. He had also chiseled the names of paternal ancestors on stone tablets and placed them in the courtyard.

On the outer wall of the Tower were figures representing aspects of the human psyche which he had identified. Standing near the Tower was a block of stone with inscriptions on three sides. For the most part the inscriptions were quotations from alchemy and they cryptically expressed the meaning of the Tower for Jung.

On one side of the stone was the figure of a small man, an image of the hidden self, who, according to the inscription, "roams through the dark regions of this cosmos and glows like a star out of the depths. He points the way to the gates of the sun and to the land of dreams."[19]

And at the bottom of one inscription he chiseled in Latin, "In remembrance of his seventy-fifth birthday C.G. Jung made and placed this here as a thanks offering, in the year 1950."[20]

The Tower was obviously a place of pilgrimage for Jung. In it he opened himself to the center and symbolized his journey in the very stones at Bollingen. Our group could not help but be struck by Jung's lifelong serious and sensitive probing of the mystery underlying human existence.

As we left the Tower to continue to Einsiedeln, it was my sense, and I am sure it was shared by others, that the Shrine and the Tower involved the same journey. In each place, with differing images and names, God was circled. Jung once observed: "Often one has the impression that the personal psyche is running round this central point like a shy animal, at once fascinated and frightened, always in flight, and yet steadily drawing nearer."[21]

Historical Notes: The Carmelites and Teresa's Reform

These next two sections contain historical material which serves as a general background for *The Interior Castle*. This first section discusses the Carmelite Order and Teresa's reform activity within that Order. The following section situates Teresa in the Spain of her times, with an emphasis on Spain's efforts in the New World.

Teresa's "Towers" were the convents she founded in an effort to provide prayerful atmospheres in simple living conditions. The Carmelite convent of the Incarnation in Avila was Teresa's introduction to the Order of Carmel. The atmosphere of the Incarnation was a busy one, although not dissolute. One hundred and eighty nuns lived there and the enclosure was not strict. Teresa found many exemplary religious in the convent, and she noted that all religious observances were kept. But she began to feel the need for a simpler, more enclosed situation.

Teresa's father, Don Alonso, died on Christmas Eve, 1543. It was a difficult time for her. "In losing him I was losing every good and joy, and he was everything to me. . . ."[22] At the same time she had been living her religious life in tension, attempting to balance contradictory interests. She wrote:

> I voyaged on this tempestuous sea for almost twenty years with these fallings and risings and this evil— since I fell again—and in a life so beneath perfection that I paid almost no attention to venial sins. And mortal sins, although I feared them, I did not fear them as I should have since I did not turn away from the dangers. I should say that it is one of the most painful lives, I think, that one can imagine; for neither did I enjoy God nor did I find happiness in the world. When I was experiencing the enjoyments of the world, I felt sorrow when I recalled what I owed to God. When I was with God, my attachments to the world disturbed me. This is a war so troublesome that I don't know how I was able to suffer it even a month, much less for so many years.[23]

Teresa was 39 years old when she experienced a "second conversion" which set her on a course allowing an ever-deepening relationship with God. A copy of St. Augustine's *Confessions* moved her: "When I came to the passage where he speaks about his conversion and read how he heard that voice in the garden, it only seemed to me, according to what I felt in my heart, that it was I the Lord called."[24]

About the same time, in 1554, she had this experience:

> It happened to me that one day entering the oratory I saw a statue they had borrowed for a certain feast to be celebrated in the house. It represented the much wounded Christ and was very devotional so that beholding it I was utterly distressed in seeing Him that way, for it well represented what He suffered for us. I felt so keenly aware of how poorly I thanked Him for those wounds that, it seems to me, my heart broke. Beseeching Him to strengthen me once and for all that I

might not offend Him, I threw myself down before Him with the greatest outpouring of tears. . . .

I think I then said that I would not rise from there until He granted what I was begging Him for. I believe certainly this was beneficial to me, because from that time I went on improving.[25]

Teresa and a group of friends and relatives began to dream of their own reformed convent. Teresa felt that the solitude and prayer which were hallmarks of Carmel suffered at the Incarnation. The travels of the nuns militated against the necessary reflection, and she was anxious about the comfort of her convent. Teresa had an increased desire for a more enclosed, prayerful, rigorous life.

The Carmelites of her day were living a mitigated, or modified, Rule of life. Teresa wished to return to what she knew as the "first" or "primitive" Rule of the Order. In actuality the Rule to which Teresa wished to return was not the first Rule of Carmel. That Rule is not known in its completeness.

The first Rule of the Carmelite Order was written sometime between 1206 and 1214 by Albert of Vercelli, Patriarch of Jerusalem. It was written at the request of a group of hermits living on Mount Carmel on the southern side of the Bay of Haifa. At the time Mount Carmel was part of the Latin Kingdom of Jerusalem established by the Crusaders. The hermits had gathered near the Well of Elias about two miles south of the promontory. The figure of Elias would become integral to Carmel's spirit.

The Rule decreed that each have his own cell and that he remain in or near it meditating on the law of the Lord day and night. There was to be a superior. Common practices of fasting and prayer were prescribed, and they would come together for Mass. Pope Honorius III confirmed this mode of life in 1226.

Saracen activity soon forced the Carmelites to leave Mount Carmel, many returning to their native countries. The earliest foundations in Western Europe were in Cyprus, Sicily, Aylesford and Hulne in England, and Les Aygalade near Marseilles in Provence.

In 1247 Pope Innocent IV published a modified Rule for the Order, allowing it to take its place as a Mendicant Order. Among its more notable changes, the new mitigated Rule allowed foundations in cities, and common meals, and it prescribed the canonical Office.

This Rule, a mitigated one, is the Rule Teresa refers to as the "Primitive" Rule. Through the mitigated Rule of 1247 we can only guess at the original Rule of Albert. The Spanish translation of the mitigated Rule led Teresa to believe it was "without mitigation."[26]

Teresa's reform of Carmel slowly became a reality with the establishment in 1562 of the first reformed convent, St. Joseph's in Avila. Last minute assistance with funds came from her brother Lorenzo in South America. The sisters, limited to no more than thirteen, shared all in common with no class distinctions as there had been at the Incarnation. Teresa developed a small, viable community structure which also contained the prayerful solitude of the eremetical life of the first Carmelities living on the slopes of Mount Carmel.

Teresa lived at St. Joseph's for the next four and a half years, calling them the most restful years of her life. Here she finished her autobiography and wrote a book for her sisters about prayer, the *Way of Perfection*.

She was encouraged to spread her reform by the General of the Order, John Rossi. An added motivation came with the visit of a Franciscan missionary from Peru who spoke of the efforts of the missionaries with the Indians. Teresa envisioned her convents as places of prayer fueling the work in the New World as well as the work of the Counter-Reformation now underway in Europe.

In the next four years Teresa founded seven convents. By the end of her life she had founded fourteen convents. Through her relationship with John of the Cross the reform took hold among the men also. Her work, the *Foundations*, tells of her efforts after the beginnings in St. Joseph's.

At the age of sixty-two, and at the request of Fr. Jerome Gratian, an enthusiastic supporter of her reform, Teresa wrote *The Interior Castle*. For five years she had been experiencing the deep union with God which she describes in the last dwelling place.

Teresa's inner pilgrimage found expression in the convents of her reform. These convents were the free and protected spaces mirroring the inner castle and providing the contemplative atmosphere for entering within. From the cave of Elias, to the cells of the first hermits on Mount Carmel, to the convents of Teresa, external "castles" have been important in the pilgrimage to the center and God.

One present-day Carmelite convent stands out in my mind. I came upon this convent while visiting the Nazi concentration camp at Dachau, outside of Munich.

Dachau is testimony to the demons that attack the human psyche. The barren, silent camp is an image of the wasteland, the meaninglessness of much of contemporary living. As I walked the camp, the scenes conjured up by the imagination were overwhelming. The silence in the camp actually screamed for answers, for explanations, for meaning.

In the back of the camp, behind three chapels built as memorials, there is a door in the wall and over the door is the sign, "Carmel of the Holy Blood." The door leads into the courtyard of a Carmelite convent which is now permanently attached to the concentration camp. In this place women live the life of solitude, prayer, and community begun at St. Joseph's in Avila four hundred years ago.

The Carmel is as quiet as the camp. No answers are given to relieve the visitors' anxiety. No explanations are given for the human behavior in the camp. There is only a prayerful attentiveness to God. The contemplation of God is based on a faith in God's love and goodness. Full healing and complete meaning come, ultimately, only from God at the center.

The journey through the inner castle is once more being made on the very site which, as much as any other image, stands for the bankruptcy of a world that has lost its soul.

An inscription over the door of Jung's home in Kusnacht is an expression of the faith found today at Dachau: "Called or not called, God will be there."

Historical Notes: The New World and a Lost City

Teresa's use of a castle as a dominant symbol for her life of prayer brings to mind the Spain of her day, a land of castles and conquests. This section will briefly situate Teresa in her times. We especially will review Spain's efforts to build an empire in the New World.

Teresa was most interested in the New World, and she was connected with this conquest through her brothers. An ironic comparison can be made between her journey to the center of an inner castle, and Spain's drive to conquer and Christianize the New World. Teresa approached the inner journey with the same sense of adventure and the same Spanish temperament as found in her brothers and their service of Spain. If she had not been a woman she might well have joined her brothers.

The final part of this section is an extended description of a "lost city" in Peru, a city never found by the Spaniards. It gives me an opportunity to develop the comparison of Teresa's exploration of an inner world while her country voyaged across oceans in outer explorations. The theme of the sacredness and call of the center continues to be a guide for these reflections.

The town of Avila was the geographical center of Spain. And Spain, during Teresa's lifetime and into the next century, was at the peak of its power and prestige. In 1492, shortly before Teresa's birth in 1515, the Moors had finally been driven from Granada after a ten year war. It was the final phase of an eight hundred year effort to reconquer Spain after the Moorish invasion.

With the capture of Granada, Spain became united under Ferdinand and Isabella. In that same year Columbus landed on islands off the coast of Central America opening a new world for Spanish exploration and expansion. The Indies, as the New World was known in Spain, attracted enormous attention and energy. And the families of Avila would contribute sons to the enterprise.

Two years before Teresa's birth, a Spanish expedition under Vasco Núñez de Balboa sighted the Pacific Ocean. In that same year of 1513 Ponce de Leon explored Florida. Juan Diaz de Solis located the Plata River in South America in 1516. Teresa's brother Rodrigo would be killed near this river fighting Arau-canos Indians.[27] Rodrigo was Teresa's favorite and the one with whom she planned childhood martyrdoms in campaigns against the Moors.

Four years after Teresa's birth, Magellan began a journey around the southern tip of South America which eventually would become the first successful navigation around the globe. After three years, the expedition arrived back in Spain, minus Magellan who had been killed in a native war in the Philippines.

The Age of Conquest began in earnest in 1519 when Cortes led a small force of Spaniards onto mainland Mexico. The Az-tecs under Montezuma II had dominated the territory. Their capital, Tenochtitlan, the site of modern Mexico City, was founded in the fourteenth century on an artificial island in the valley lake. This capital, and the Aztec empire, fell in a Spanish attack by boat and over causeways in the summer of 1521.

The rebuilt city became the capital of a Spanish territory extending south into Central America and north to the Gulf of California. The energy of the Spaniards was such that by 1540–42 an expedition under Vasquez de Coronado penetrated as far as modern Kansas.

The Mayan civilization in the Yucatan peninsula and in parts of Guatemala proved more difficult to dominate than the Aztecs. Not until 1545 was the Yucatan peninsula in firm Span-ish control.

Meanwhile other Spanish conquest armies moved into South America and especially Peru. Shortly before Teresa en-tered the convent of the Incarnation, the Spanish invaded the Inca empire high in the Andes mountains. Sailing from Panama in 1531 Francisco Pizarro landed at Tumbez on the Pacific coast and marched south and east toward Cuzco, the capital city of the Incas.

In invading the Incas, or really the Quechua people who were later given the name of their ruler the Inca, the Spaniards were coming in contact with the most developed social and political system in all native America. The Inca domain centered on Cuzco, which literally meant "navel." The Incas had gold and silver in abundance, using it simply for decoration.

The Incas worshiped the sun. Garcilaso de la Vega, son of a Spanish father and an Inca princess, recorded their legend in 1609. According to the legend people were living like wild beasts:

Seeing the condition they were in, our father the Sun was ashamed for them, and he decided to send one of his sons and one of his daughters from heaven and earth, in order that they might teach men to adore him and acknowledge him as their god. . . .

Our father the Sun set his two children down at a place eighty leagues from here, on Lake Titicaca, and he gave them a rod of gold, a little shorter than a man's arm and two fingers in thickness.

"Go where you will," he said to them, "and whenever you stop to eat or to sleep, plunge this rod into the earth. At the spot where, with one single thrust, it disappears entirely, there you must establish and hold your court. . . ."

"To the entire world," added our father the Sun, "I give my light and my brilliance; I give men warmth when they are cold; I cause their fields to fructify and their cattle to multiply; each day that passes I go all around the world in order to have a better knowledge of men's needs and to satisfy these needs: follow my example. . . ."

Having thus declared his will to his two children, our father the Sun dismissed them. They then left Lake Titicaca and walked northwards, trying vainly each day to thrust their rod of gold into the earth. . . . The Inca and his bride, our queen, entered into Cuzco valley which, at that time, was nothing but wild, mountainous country.[28]

The Spanish conquistadors found a Temple of the Sun in Cuzco when they invaded in 1532. The empire fell in one year. Teresa's older brother Hernando, her mother's first son, entered Peru with an expedition under Hernando Pizarro. In the years to come, Lorenzo, closest to his sister next to Rodrigo, and Jeronimo, another favorite, would both land in Peru to find their share of excitement and wealth. Lorenzo helped finance St. Joseph's, Teresa's first convent of the reform. At propitious moments the gold of Peru would further Teresa's efforts.

For forty years after the fall of Cuzco, the Spanish struggled to remove any possible renewal of Inca leadership. Expeditions scoured the mountains and ranged the course of the Sacred Valley of the Incas in pursuit of opposition.

The Incas were accomplished stone-workers and architects, and they built lofty fortresses with immensely heavy stones. These fortresses were their retreats when they were driven from Cuzco. But, in time, the Spaniards penetrated into these remote places and in 1572, just ten years before Teresa's death, Tupac Amaru, the last supposed heir to the role of Inca, was captured and killed.

Centuries passed and the story continues again in our own time.

In 1911 Hiram Bingham, an American professor, led a Yale University expedition from Cuzco into the Sacred Valley of the Incas in search of a lost city hinted at in historical records. Following the Urubamba River, an important affluent of the mighty Amazon River, the expedition moved past ancient Incan watch-towers, terraces, and fortresses.

Seventy-five miles from Cuzco the Yale professor made camp in a rainstorm at the base of a steep ridge. In the morning, with the aid of a local Indian guide, Bingham's party located at the top of the ridge between two mountains a city which would become known as Machu Picchu.

Surrounded on three sides by the Urubamba River two thousand feet below, and protected by the mountain of Machu Picchu on the fourth side, the city had been lost to memory. With the exception of a few local Indians, Machu Picchu was totally unknown to Peruvians themselves. Access to the valley had been so difficult and the city so invisible from the valley floor that centuries went by without a hint of its existence reaching the outside world. As Bingham wrote, the city was located "in the most inaccessible corner of the most inaccessible section of the central Andes."[29]

The stone walls were in perfect condition; only the thatched roofs were missing. The various sections of the city were connected by stairways, one hundred in all, which crossed in every direction. Long agricultural terraces were nearby. The city had fountains and squares and beautifully constructed temples.

The temples adjoined a "Sacred Plaza." On the western end of this ceremonial terrace rose a pyramid of fourteen platforms covered by grass. One edge of the pyramid plunged straight down to the river deep in the canyon.

At the top of the pyramid, the highest point in the city, Bingham found the mysterious stone called the Intihuatana. Similar stones had been found in Peru, and it was assumed that they were involved in the religious rituals of the Incas. This central point was probably a type of solar observatory involved in the worship of the sun, "Inti." One tradition says that in the darkest days of the winter solstice the Incas "tethered" the sun to the stone to keep it from disappearing altogether.

The exact nature of life in Machu Picchu remains a mystery. The Incas had no written records. Whether the entire city was considered a sacred place or just the temple and pyramid area is a question. Of the one hundred and seventy-three mummies found by the Yale expedition, one hundred and fifty were young women. This fact led Bingham to speculate that the last residents of Machu Picchu were "Chosen Women," the virgins who were associated with sun worship. They, perhaps, had fled from Cuzco to this sanctuary.

The story of Machu Picchu interests me for several reasons. The mandala form of the pyramid with the stone at the center adds confirmation to the sacredness of "centering" whether on a physical or a psychological plane. Mircea Eliade's words are as illuminative of Machu Picchu as they are of Dora Kalff's sand tray, the Shrine of the Black Madonna, Jung's Tower, Teresa's convents and Mount Carmel itself:

> This multivalency, this applicability to multiple although closely comparable planes, is a characteristic of the symbolism of the Centre in general. This is easily understandable, since every human being tends, even unconsciously, towards the Centre, and towards his own centre, where he can find integral reality—sacredness. This desire, so deeply rooted in man, to find himself at the very heart of the real—at the Centre of the World, the place of communication with Heaven—explains the ubiquitous use of "Centres of the World". . . . So that all houses—like all temples, palaces and cities— are situated at one and the same point, the Centre of the Universe.[30]

Machu Picchu, suspended in the clouds between two peaks, makes a visually striking claim to being at the center of the universe, the place of communication with the heavens. The city links itself with the sun, the source of light and warmth in the Andes, and its inhabitants find their meaning and identity as people of the sun.

The very description of the Incas' citadel brings to mind Teresa's inner castle. Each has different levels, a multitude of rooms, gardens, fountains and a center related to a divine presence.

The physical proximity of Teresa's brothers to this sanctuary forms a connection leading all the way back to Spain and the convent enclosures. Her brother Hernando had possibly entered the Sacred Valley of the Incas with the forces of Hernando Pizarro. Pizarro fought a major battle with the Incas at Ollantaytambo, a fortress on the way to Machu Picchu.

But the Spanish never found Machu Picchu. Excavations have produced no evidence of Spanish influence or even temporary presence. Their written records make no mention of Machu Picchu. Indifferent to hardships, determined, and often fatalistic, the soldiers demonstrated combinations of honorable and base conduct, of altruism and selfishness. The Spanish monarchy had accepted, with Papal confirmation, the duty of Christianizing the Indians, but the relationship of this goal to outright conquest became more and more questionable. I find irony in the fact that the conquistadors, with all their energy and resourcefulness, never located this Incan sanctuary.

On the other hand, Teresa's adventure during the years of the Conquest was the inner effort recounted in *The Interior Castle*. She entered this realm with no less energy than her brothers demonstrated in entering the New World. But her goal was the Christianizing of Teresa. She learned that the true center can only be discovered when it reveals itself and on its own terms.

The Incas recognized a power in their lives upon which they depended, and attributed it to the sun. Jung found the sun symbolic of the center to which the personality is drawn and by which it is nourished. Teresa named the mystery at the center God, God who called her to a union for the fullness of light and warmth, of life and meaning.

Both the lost city of the Incas and the inner castle of Teresa are "far countries." Most people need a "far country" to which they can travel, if only in imagination, and there set about discovering their lost souls.

Teresa opens the mind's eye to the expanse of such an inner world:

> Well now let's get back to our castle with its many dwelling places. You mustn't think of these dwelling places in such a way that each one would follow in file after the other; but turn your eyes toward the center, which is the room or royal chamber where the King stays, and think of how a palmetto has many leaves surrounding and covering the tasty part that can be eaten. So here, surrounding this center room, are many other rooms; and the same holds true for those above. The things of the soul must always be considered as plentiful, spacious, and large; to do so is not an exaggeration. The soul is capable of much more than we can imagine, and the sun that is in this royal chamber shines in all

parts. It is very important for any soul that practices prayer, whether little or much, not to hold itself back and stay in one corner. Let it walk through these dwelling places which are up above, down below, and to the sides, since God has given it such great dignity.[31]

Concluding Reflections and Suggestions

Carl Jung's theories and Teresa of Avila's process in *The Interior Castle* strongly suggest that we attempt to tell our story. The telling of our story requires that we image our experience. The images may become symbols which point to the sacred levels in our lives where God contacts us and calls us to life.

This first image of the castle suggests that we could begin our story by finding a predominant image, or several major images. These images will be ones which appear to powerfully affect us or draw us. They will provide a context, a container for our story.

These predominant images will give unity and flow to other images in our lives, sub-symbols relating to our experience. Often these images have been with us a long time, but we have never reflected upon them or allowed them to speak to us.

Following Teresa's suggestion of entering the castle and walking around in it, I can enter my symbols of wholeness and walk around in them through active imagination. Active imagination is a process of engaging a symbol in some way. I may write it down with a full description, or I may draw, sketch, or diagram it. I could dialogue with it in a spontaneous fashion, allowing two points of view to emerge. The image could become the starting point for an imaginative story which I weave around it. All of these processes are ways of helping me hear my depths through the imagery of my life. Jung's theories relating to this process will be more completely developed in a later chapter.

The predominant image of wholeness will center me and provide a free, protected space where I may play with my life. A powerful image which addresses the core of my personhood will help reconstellate the self, put me in touch with my wider life.

Sometimes positive childhood memories can be the beginning of contacting the self once again.

Some people draw mandalas. It is a simple process. Lightly draw a circle approximately the size of a face. Be mindful that there is a center to the circle, and then simply begin to color and draw within the circle. There are no rules. It is a free space for play. When finished, turn the mandala around until you are satisfied you have found a top and bottom. Then write down comments about it, whatever comes to mind. Or reflect on it with another. If the mandala strikes you, you may want to hang it up and live with it awhile.

I know a chaplain who holds monthly reflection sessions for inmates in a women's prison. As part of the reflection session the inmates are offered the opportunity to draw mandalas. The chaplain reports that a number of the inmates enjoy being able to express themselves in the drawing and coloring. The space of the mandala is one of the few areas of life where they feel control.

When the mandalas are finished the chaplain asks if anyone would like to talk about the mandala she has drawn. A number of the inmates do have comments and the comments begin to reveal where they are in the story of their life. This beginning reflection on their experience often leads to further discussions with the chaplain. The chaplain says that the mandala activity of the inmates provides her with insights as she attempts to be more responsive and sensitive in her ministry.

Teresa and Jung had their convent and Tower as environments for their inner storying. Do I need a building, a room, or an outdoor spot where I can be centered? Is there a place I can be where my mind roams, life sorts itself out, and I can feel connected? Is it also a place where I can just be attentive to mystery, to God in my life, without a thought or an image? Such an environment is invaluable for its power to heal and renew me.

We might think about making a pilgrimage. This suggestion is rooted in the conviction that *The Interior Castle* is an inner pilgrimage. A pilgrimage in space and time may aid the inner journey. Pilgrimages lead to sacred places where the human and divine meet. We each have our own sacred places which could become centers of pilgrimage. I can visit my birthplace, or the birthplaces of others who are significant in my life. Family graves are places of sacredness. Marriage vows and religious life vows have hallowed places. Childhood scenes, places of healing, and spots where God's presence was deeply experienced can be destinations for pilgrimage. I leave home, close the door on what is familiar, and journey to a place where I am open to God's touch once more. The distance I travel is not important. I am on pilgrimage and all pilgrimage is an opening to the same center. Teresa of Avila ultimately locates that center within us, where we meet God and come to know ourselves fully.

NOTES

1. Jung, C.W., IXi, 713.
2. Ibid., 646.
3. Jung, *Memories*, p. 196.
4. Jung, C.W., IXi. In this volume, too, is a mandala painted by Jung which is strikingly similar to Teresa's castle. Jung provides this description: "Painting of a medieval city with walls and moats, streets and churches, arranged quadratically. The inner city is again surrounded by walls and moats, like the Imperial City in Peking. The buildings all open inwards, towards the centre, represented by a castle with a golden roof. It too is surrounded by a moat. The ground round the castle is laid with black and white tiles, representing the united opposites. . . . A picture like this is not unknown in Christian symbolism" (p. 377).
5. *Interior Castle*, I, chap. 1, no. 1.
6. Ibid., p. 20.
7. Ibid., Epilogue, no. 1.
8. Ibid., I, chap. 1, no. 5.
9. Jung, *Memories*, pp. 197, 8.
10. Ibid., pp. 198, 9.
11. Victor Turner and Edith Turner, *Image and Pilgrimage in Christian Culture* (New York: Columbia University Press, 1978), pp. 33, 4.
12. *Interior Castle*, Epilogue, no. 3.
13. Jung, C.W., VIII, 696.
14. Jung, C.W., XVIII, 625–8.

15. Jung, *Memories*, p. 223.

16. Ibid., p. 224.

17. Ibid., pp. 225, 226.

18. Ibid., p. 224.

19. Ibid., p. 227.

20. Ibid., p. 228.

21. Jung, C.W., XII, 326.

22. Teresa of Avila, *The Book of Her Life* in *The Collected Works of St. Teresa of Avila*, vol. I, trans. Kieran Kavanaugh and Otilio Rodriguez (Washington, D.C.: Institute of Carmelite Studies, 1976), chap. 7, no. 14.

23. Ibid., chap. 8, no. 2.

24. Ibid., chap. 9, no. 8.

25. Ibid., chap. 9, nos. 1, 3.

26. For a discussion of Teresa's reform of Carmel see Joachim Smet, *The Carmelites*, vol. II (Darien, Ill.: Carmelite Spiritual Center, 1976), pp. 22ff. For a recent biography of Teresa see Stephen Clissold, *St. Teresa of Avila* (London: Sheldon Press, 1979).

27. For information on Teresa's brothers in South America see Efren de la Madre de Dios and Otger Steggink, *Tiempo Y Vida De Santa Teresa* (Madrid: BAC, 1977), pp. 56–8.

28. Garcilaso de la Vega, *The Incas*, trans. Maria Jolas (New York: Avon Books, Discus Edition, 1971), pp. 43, 4.

29. See Hiram Bingham, *Machu Picchu, A Citadel of the Incas* (New York: Hacker Art Books, 1979).

30. Mircea Eliade, *Images and Symbols* (New York: Sheed and Ward, 1969), p. 54.

31. *Interior Castle*, I, chap. 2, no. 8.

CHAPTER THREE

The Deep Waters of the Inner World

Our unknown inner world invites exploration and discovery. The mystery lying at the heart of creation is present within our depths continually surprising and challenging us. The God at the core of our being acts as an inexhaustible spring flowing into our lives.

In our day we are well aware that much of the story of our lives is hidden from our consciousness. It is taking place in the unconscious. Teresa uses water to image the deep movements of God within her. Carl Jung found that the same image of water expressed the unknown part of the human psyche, the unconscious.

Water as a Symbol for the Unconscious

Water had a powerful effect on Jung, as it did on Teresa. In the beginning of his autobiography he tells of his early memories of water:

> My mother took me to the Thurgau to visit friends, who had a castle on Lake Constance. I could not be dragged away from the water. The waves from the steamer washed up to the shore, the sun glistened on the water, and the sand under the water had been curled into little ridges by the waves. The lake

stretched away and away into the distance. This expanse of water was an inconceivable pleasure to me, an
incomparable splendor. At that time the idea became
fixed in my mind that I must live near a lake; without
water, I thought, nobody could live at all.[1]

Both his house in Kusnacht and his Tower at Bollingen were
built on the lake.

Later, in his psychological practice and studies, water became a most familiar symbol. In Jung's estimation, water is the
most common symbol for the unconscious.[2] As an example, he
quoted a patient's report of his dreams: "Almost every time I
dream it is about water: either I am having a bath, or the water-
closet is overflowing, or a pipe is bursting, or my home has
drifted down to the water's edge, or I see an acquaintance about
to sink into water, or I am trying to get out of water, or I am
having a bath and the tub is about to overflow."[3] If water is
symbolic of the unconscious, then this somewhat humorous lit-
any certainly seems to indicate a stirring of the unconscious.

The entrance into one's unconscious is often imaged as entrance into water. Or the flooding of consciousness by the unconscious may be imaged as a flood of water in some form.
Psychologically, water refers to spirit that has become unconscious. It does not, then, mean a regression to an inferior life but
a descent to depths where there is a possibility for nourishment.
Healing and new life can be the result of entering these waters.
The waters of baptism are certainly meant to symbolize this
transformation. The descent is necessary before there can be an
ascent. Jung tells of a dream of a theologian:

[The theologian] dreamed that he saw on a mountain a
kind of Castle of the Grail. He went along a road that
seemed to lead straight to the foot of the mountain and
up it. But as he drew nearer he discovered to his great
disappointment that a chasm separated him from the
mountain, a deep, darksome gorge with underworldly
water rushing along the bottom. A steep path led
downwards and toilsomely climbed up again on the

other side. But the prospect looked uninviting, and the dreamer awoke.[4]

Jung comments that the dreamer, in order to reach the Castle on the heights, had to descend into the depths first.

Similarly, the journey to the center of the castle, for Teresa, required entering powerful and unknown depths within oneself. Quite understandably, water presented itself as an image of that hidden world. Deep waters contain life which is invisible to surface eyes, and on the bottom rest wrecks and treasure for the finding. It is no wonder the psyche views water as symbolic of the unconscious.

Notes taken during one of Jung's seminars contain the following thoughts on water symbolism:

> Whenever water appears it is usually the water of life, meaning a medium through which one is reborn. It symbolizes a sort of baptism ceremony, or initiation, a healing bath that gives resurrection or rebirth. . . .
>
> The baptismal font . . . is the return to the womb of consciousness, since consciousness has arisen in that state. . . . The return to such a condition has healing value, because it brings things back to their origin, where nothing is disturbed, yet everything is still right. It is as if one were gaining there a sort of orientation of how things really ought to be. . . . Return into the mandala is something like a sleep or a trance in which the conscious is done away with to a large extent and things can find their natural way again. And the water is healing simply because it is the low condition of consciousness where everything is undisturbed and can therefore fall into the right rhythm.[5]

The Reality of the Unconscious

To say that water is a symbol of the unconscious is to accept a fundamental tenet of depth psychology, that is, the existence of the unconscious. The unconscious has been connected, rightfully, with Sigmund Freud, the founder of modern depth psychology. However, a concept such as the unconscious can only be part of a stream of thinking extending back centuries into human history. Freud added empirical data to a theory which had been rumored from time immemorial. The extreme concentration on self-consciousness found in Cartesian dualism and the relegation of all else to the physical, material world set the stage for a reaction of the unconscious.

If conscious is used to mean immediately known to awareness, the unconscious is used to mean all other mental processes. It is a negative concept, hardly descriptive, but carries the connotation that the mental process is one, and that only a small part of this process ever reaches the awareness of the person.

The reaction of the unconscious to stress on self-consciousness can be found in Romanticism, and it is in this period that the unconscious began to be formally recognized. L.L. Whyte, in his study, *The Unconscious Before Freud,* examines two hundred years of European interest in the unconscious, from approximately 1680 to 1880. He maintains, ". . . the idea of the unconscious mental processes was, in many of its aspects, conceivable around 1700, topical around 1800, and became effective around 1900. . . ."[6]

The English word "unconscious" first appears in 1751. England and Germany dealt with the terms conscious and unconscious before they became part of French writings. They were first used in Germany by E. Platner in 1776, and similar terms were used by Goethe, Schiller, and Schelling between 1780 and 1820. Whyte maintains that in the thirty years prior to Freud there were ten to twenty writers in each decade who made a minor contribution to the notion of the unconscious.

Two prime examples of concern with the unconscious before Freud are C.G. Carus (1789–1869) and Eduard von Hartmann (1842–1906). Carus, a German physician and friend of Goethe, stated that the aim of human life and growth should be the making conscious of the unconscious. He maintained that consciousness was personal, and the unconscious was supra-individual, sleepless, and untiring. He wrote: "The highest aspiration of the conscious mind, the attainment of God, can be approached only by its submission to the deepest depths of what to us is purely unconscious."[7]

Von Hartmann wrote *Philosophy of the Unconscious* (1868) which was a survey of German and Western science interpreted in the light of unconscious mental processes. It was an immense work, and its existence demonstrates that when Freud was twelve years old, twenty-six aspects of unconscious mental activity had been considered in detail in a famous work.

The Waters of the Castle

Teresa herself attests to the symbolic nature of water in *The Interior Castle*. Water has a long history in her life. She writes: "For I don't find anything more appropriate to explain some spiritual experiences than water; and this is because I know little and have no helpful cleverness of mind and am so fond of this element that I have observed it more attentively than other things. . . . I believe that in each little thing created by God there is more than what is understood, even if it is a little ant."[8]

Water has such an attraction for Teresa that she uses it as an image for the entire life of the spirit. God contacts the soul in the depths of life. In particular, water becomes her expression of a fundamental distinction between two types of prayer which are experienced in the castle. The first type is prayer of active meditation and it is the prayer of the first three dwelling places. The second type of prayer is a supernatural, infused prayer that is characteristic of the last three dwelling places. The middle dwelling place, the fourth, is the place of transition. It is in this fourth dwelling place that Teresa locates her example of the two fonts with two water troughs: "These two troughs are filled with water in different ways; with one the water comes from far away through many aqueducts and the use of much ingenuity; with the other the source of the water is right there, and the trough fills without any noise. If the spring is abundant, as is this one we are speaking about, the water overflows once the trough is filled, forming a large stream. There is no need of any skill, nor does the building of aqueducts have to continue; but water is always flowing from the spring."[9]

The trough that is filled by aqueducts represents prayer that begins with the person and ends in God. The person, with God's grace, initiates the effort and sustains it through a controlled use of imagination, memory, thought and prayerful expression. It is active meditation and the water represents the consolations (*contentos*), such as joy and peace, which are the result of such natural effort.

The trough that is filled directly from the spring represents prayer that begins with God and ends in the person. It is supernatural, infused prayer. God is the source of this water and it represents the spiritual delights (*gustos*) which are infused experiences. She writes: "He produces this delight with the greatest peace and quiet and sweetness in the very interior part of ourselves. I don't know from where or how, nor is that happiness and delight experienced as are earthly consolations in the heart. I mean there is no similarity at the beginning, for afterward the delight fills everything; this water overflows through all the dwelling places and faculties until reaching the body. That is why I said that it begins in God and ends in ourselves."[10] In other words, the fourth dwelling place is the beginning of true mystical prayer which deepens and expands through the remaining dwelling places.

By the time Teresa describes the experiences of the sixth dwelling place, the fountain waters have become an ocean:

> It seems that the trough of water we mentioned (I believe it was in the fourth dwelling place, for I don't recall exactly) filled so easily and gently, I mean without any movement. Here this great God, who holds back the springs of water and doesn't allow the sea to go beyond its boundaries, lets loose the springs from which the water in this trough flows. With a powerful impulse, a huge wave rises up so forcefully that it lifts high this little bark that is our soul. A bark cannot prevent the furious waves from leaving it where they will; nor does the pilot have the power, nor do those who take part in controlling the little ship. So much less can

the interior part of the soul stay where it will, or make its senses or faculties do other than what they are commanded; here the soul doesn't care what happens outwardly.[11]

Because of her experiences of God's action in her soul, Teresa uses water to convey the sense of hidden riches and depths within the human person. The use of water is an attempt to express the psychological effects of God's activity in her. Water depicts her awareness of the deep, interior presence of God. As a symbolic expression, we might even say that water chose itself to represent these experiences, since it had such a powerful attraction for Teresa.

Teresa's writings, and especially this image of water, are a creative attempt to shed light on the subtleties of human interiority. She is an early psychologist describing the development of the human person under the action of God. "For certainly," she writes, "I see secrets within ourselves that have often caused me to marvel . . . for even in our own selves there are great secrets that we don't understand."[12]

The Interior Castle, then, is a document of the psyche as well as the soul. Because psyche and soul refer to human interiority they are often used interchangeably. Certain writers today will simply refer to psyche, and mean by it all that soul meant. However, even though both designate the essence of the human self, distinctions can be made between the two which do justice to both psychology and religion. In general, the psyche can be said to refer to the functions within the human personality, the conscious and unconscious dimensions of that personality, and the relationship of that personality to others. The soul, on the other hand, refers to the meeting of that personality, that human life, with the divine. The soul is that dimension of interiority which links the individual with its ultimate source in God.[13]

Teresa's use of soul is inclusive of what today is referred to as psyche. Scholastic theology spoke of faculties of powers within the soul in an attempt to psychologically nuance inner reality. Teresa attempts to overcome a lack of psychological categories through her use of imagery. The water image is an example of her ability to compensate for an underdeveloped psychology. No psychological system, however, would be able to capture her experiences and adequately convey them. Symbols would always be necessary for her ineffable experiences. In the seventh dwelling place Teresa even nuances her use of soul when she says that the union of the mystical marriage takes place in a superior part of the soul, the spirit.

The Psyche According to C.G. Jung

The image of water and its evocation of the depths of the psyche points to the more detailed mapping of human interiority found in modern depth psychology. The findings of depth psychology provide us with an advantage which Teresa did not enjoy, but an advantage she would have greatly appreciated. Since this study of Teresa is also meant to be an introduction to Carl Jung, the following information is offered as beginning orientation to Jung's theories concerning the psyche. The human psyche was the focus of his long labor. "Psychology," he wrote, "is neither biology nor physiology nor any other science than just this knowledge of the psyche."[14]

The *psyche* refers to the totality of the personality. It is a spaceless space, an inner cosmos which incorporates all psychic processes, conscious as well as unconscious. The psyche has an inherent wholeness which has to be recovered and developed.

Consciousness is that part of the psyche known directly by the individual. It consists of the thoughts, memories, and feelings which are present in one's awareness. In relationship to the unconscious, consciousness is the smaller part of the psyche.

The *ego* is the center of consciousness. It is the gatekeeper to consciousness since experiences of the outer and inner worlds must pass through the ego in order to be conscious. Of the overwhelming number of daily experiences in an individual's life, the ego allows only a portion to filter into consciousness. It is an island of identity and continuity for the personality. A healthy ego-consciousness is an important goal in human development.

The psyche has within its space *energy* or *libido*. Psychic energy moves throughout the space of the psyche and does the work of the personality. Jung used the terms libido and energy interchangeably. But he used libido in a wider sense than did Freud who restricted it to sexual energy. For Jung, libido was undifferentiated energy, the energy of all the processes of life. Some of the energy is derived from the instincts, but for the most part energy is the result of experiences. Interaction with the environment generates energy within the psyche. Just as food is converted into physical life, so experience is converted into psychic energy. In these descriptions we are necessarily speaking metaphorically since we do not really know what physical and psychic energy are. But they operate "as if."

Fundamental to energy in the psyche is movement. The movement of psychic processes depends upon the *principle of opposites*. For Jung, psychic energy acts "as if" it were structured according to polarities or opposites. The principle of opposites is a way of thinking about psychic processes. Movement, even in the outer world, appears to be the result of contending forces, dynamic tension. The fact that mythologies concerning creation and the goals of peoples are often cast in terms of opposites and contrasts led Jung to view the principle of opposites as a fundamental characteristic of the psyche. The principle seems to correspond to the psyche's way of acting. The psyche's movement to harmony and wholeness is a balancing of opposites.

Jung named other principles which seem to correlate with the movement of libido. The *principle of equivalence* states that energy which disappears from one part of the psyche will reappear in another part. The psyche is a relatively closed system and, consequently, energy does not escape.

For example, many events which made a lasting impression on us are not present in our consciousness but are very much alive in our unconscious. Just because we are not aware of something does not mean that it has escaped our psyche. The energy involved has just been transferred to another part of the psyche.

Similarly, energy in the unconscious may appear in conscious activity. For example, the unconscious effects of a relationship with one person may influence our relationship with a second person. Psychologists speak of this dynamic as transference.

Another principle of psychic process is the *principle of equilibrium*. The energy represented in polarities will tend toward a balance. A movement to harmony and balance persists throughout the psyche. When one pole of a bi-polar situation has received more energy than its opposite, the energy then tends to flow into the neglected pole.

An example is the peak and trough of a wave. A law appears to be operating whereby the trough will rise and the peak will lower in order to achieve a union of these opposites. So, too, any extreme or imbalance in the psyche will cause a reaction. This principle is also known as the principle of entropy. A complete balancing, or stasis, never occurs because new energy is constantly being added as a result of new experiences.

Although energy moves in many directions, the most basic psychic process was designated by Jung as *progression* and *regression*. The libido is in a progressive movement when the psyche is balanced and energy flows out to life in a creative way. With the opposites in harmony energy is free to move forward. The progressive movement of energy is a movement up from the unconscious to conscious life.

When the balance between the opposites breaks apart then a regressive movement of energy ensues. The union of the opposites is broken when an obstacle appears, when something dams up the energy. The opposites become in conflict and more energy is generated but it is trapped within the psyche. The energy begins to move deeper into the psyche. The regressive movement of energy is a movement from consciousness into the unconscious.

Regression is not an entirely negative dynamic because it is a return to the psyche, the inner world which is calling for attention. Regression may be a sign of a disturbance but it is also the route to restoration of balance and growth in the psyche. With that renewal, the progressive movement of adaptation to the outer world may continue.

The Psyche: Personality Types

In his theory of personality types Jung identified four psychological functions: thinking, feeling, intuiting, sensing. The development of these functions corresponds to growth in consciousness and a healthy adaptation to the world. A function is a particular form of psychic activity which remains the same in principle under varying conditions. Personalities differ according to the degree of development of the various functions. Although all four functions are present in each psyche, usually one predominates. Which function predominates probably depends upon the psychic constitution of the individual.

Sensation and intuition, two irrational functions, have to do with the way whereby we perceive our experiences. A person with a highly developed *sensation function* perceives experience through the sense organs as well as through interior sensations. This function is sometimes called the reality function since it is alert to factual detail. It tells us that something exists.

The *intuition function*, on the other hand, operates almost as a "sixth sense." This function perceives almost instinctively. A content seems to present itself whole and entire. Perceptions are mediated to the intuitive function in an unconscious way. It is not as alert to the sense data, but it perceives the meaning and possibility of a situation. Whereas the sensation function tells us that something exists, the intuition function tells us where it came from and where it is going.

For example, the two functions will perceive a meeting of a group of individuals in two different ways. The sensation function will enable an individual to perceive specifics of the meeting: the overall setting, the arrangement of chairs, the clothing of the individuals, and the specific statements of individuals. The intuition function will allow a person to perceive the forces at work that led to the meeting, to sense meanings only hinted at, and to guess the possible impact of the meeting. Since the two functions are opposites, they will not be equally well-developed in the same individual.

Thinking and feeling, two rational functions, determine the manner whereby we judge, or come to conclusions about, our perceptions. The *thinking function* uses a logical process that links ideas together which then lead to a conclusion. It is an intellectual function which seeks to understand something. The *feeling function* uses a process of evaluation leading to like or dislike, acceptance or rejection. Something is accepted or rejected depending upon whether it arouses a pleasant or unpleasant feeling.

Jung considered both the thinking and feeling functions to be rational functions because they both involve evaluating and judging. The thinking function determines whether something is true or false through objective cognition. The feeling function determines whether it is pleasant or unpleasant through subjective feeling. The thinking function tells us that something is; the feeling function tells us if it is agreeable or not. Again, these functions are both rational functions but they are polar opposites and will not be developed equally in the same individual.

Along with the four psychological functions, Jung theorized that personalities differ according to two basic attitudes: *extroversion and introversion.* An extrovert's flow of energy is outward; an introvert's flow of energy is inward. This movement of energy is different from the progression and regression dynamic. Both extroversion and introversion are healthy, progressive movements of libido. In the case of the extrovert the movement is out to the objective world. The extrovert is drawn by the environment, collective norms, the spirit of the times. The extrovert invests energy in people and things outside of herself and is motivated by the surroundings.

The introvert, however, is drawn by the inner, subjective world. The introvert's cues and motivations come from within. The introvert is interested in exploring and analyzing this inner world.

The extrovert is better adapted to the environment, more outgoing and at ease with interactions around him. He appears to take a lively interest in the world. The introvert, often, is not as well adjusted to the environment. The introvert may appear withdrawn or aloof. The extrovert is characterized by a positive relation to the environment, the introvert by a negative one. The extrovert is usually eager regarding suggested activities.

The introvert responds, at first, with an unvoiced "no." After the initial negative reaction the introvert may then decide and act otherwise.

Each personality is a combination of these two attitudes but the constitution of the individual psyche determines which type predominates. The types naturally have difficulty understanding one another.

I remember the example of an extrovert and an introvert who were going to take a long car trip together. At the last minute the extrovert could not make the trip and felt badly that she would deprive the introvert of her company. But the introvert's reactions surprised her. The introvert was not that disappointed in the change of plans and adjusted quickly to the idea of making the trip alone. Somewhat hurt, the extrovert began to wonder how necessary she was to the trip in the first place. But the introvert meant nothing personal. She would have enjoyed the company, but even without the other person the introvert would have plenty to occupy her. Her own internal thoughts and reactions and musings would provide a large agenda.

The two types tend to confuse and misjudge one another. One of the more helpful distinctions I have heard states: extroverts talk to think; introverts think to talk.

In Jungian typology, then, there are a great number of personality types. Not only will people be extroverts or introverts, but they will also differ according to psychological functions. One person may be an extroverted thinking type, while another person may be an introverted feeling type. Of course, there are no "pure" types in existence, but the labels at least begin to identify traits of individual personalities.

The awareness of personality types can help us avoid unnecessary conflict, and value types different from ourselves. The two attitudes and the four functions will be developed and used in differing degrees by each person. The attitudes and functions are part and parcel with the development of personality which will be discussed in the next chapter.

The Psyche: The Unconscious

The *unconscious* refers to those aspects of personality which are not present in the awareness of the individual. The unconscious is the realm of that which is unknown within the psyche. The word itself is negative because it means the absence of consciousness, but Jung conceives of it as a positive reality. The unconscious is the source for the materials of consciousness and consequently has a creative role in the psyche.

Jung identifies two layers of the unconscious. The layer closer to consciousness he calls the *personal unconscious*. The content of the personal unconscious consists of material which at one time had been conscious. It is a realm of thoughts, memories and feelings which were known but now, for various reasons, have left consciousness and reside in the unconscious. The personal unconscious is also the location of impressions which were never quite strong enough to enter consciousness. In general, the personal unconscious develops as a result of personal experiences of the individual who is growing into consciousness.

Certain contents in the personal unconscious group together in constellations of energy which Jung called *complexes*. He discovered these formations through his word-association experiments. People were slow or hesitant in responding to certain words and Jung hypothesized that the words touched unconscious feelings which blocked a spontaneous response. These complexes act as autonomous little personalities within the psyche. They represent touchy areas which distort reality and have an attraction over the ego.

For example, someone with an inferiority complex relates all experiences to that feeling. Other people's comments and actions are perceived only from the point of view of one's own felt inferiority. But complexes are not necessarily abnormal conditions. Complexes which fuel creativity in artists have beneficial outcomes. However, when a complex, operating as a partial system within the individual, becomes too autonomous and out of relation with the rest of the psyche, then an unbalanced, disturbed condition is the result.

The deeper layer of the unconscious Jung called the *collec-*

tive unconscious. This layer differs from the personal unconscious in that its existence does not depend upon personal experience. The contents of the collective unconscious have never been conscious and are the result of heredity and evolution. We have this layer of the unconscious by being born as humans. Just as our bodies are linked with the past through the evolutionary process, so too are our psyches.

Within the collective unconscious are pre-existent forms which Jung called *archetypes.* The archetypes are primordial images common to all humankind. By "primordial image" Jung did not mean specific images or ideas, but predispositions or patterns. Archetypes have also been called channels, watercourses, and imprints. They are similar to negatives which need to be developed.

Jung arrived at the theory of archetypes as he discovered common patterns and themes in the dreams of present day patients as well as in the fairytales and mythology of history. The specifics of images and stories differed according to individuals and cultures but the underlying patterns of meaning were the same. Such studies led him to assume a transpersonal level of psyche which was fundamental for human development.

Jung named many of the archetypes found within the collective unconscious, such as birth, rebirth, death, the journey of the hero, God, the wise old man, the earth mother, and objects of nature such as the sun and moon. These and other images represent typical experiences and motifs in life and the psyche has an inherited tendency to respond to these situations and motifs with typical responses.

The archetypes provide patterns of meaning and guides to growth for the developing personality. A person's conscious experience is what gives an archetype specific content. Archetypes cannot be known in themselves. They become the nucleus of a complex drawing associated material from an individual's experience to themselves. Hopefully, the concept of an archetype will become clearer as we study the archetypes of shadow, anima, and animus later in the book, and as we now discuss the self.

The archetype of wholeness in the psyche is the *self.* The

self is the center of the personality and the circumference. It expresses the unity of the personality as a whole. The conscious and unconscious, together, form the self. It is the central archetype in the collective unconscious calling the personality to order and unity. As an objective of the psyche, the self is a goal never reached. It is a centerpoint bringing harmony and balance to the psyche. The goal of the individual is to achieve selfhood, self-realization, or, in Jung's term, individuation. This achievement necessitates a shift from ego to self as the center of the psyche.

When an archetype becomes known to consciousness, it does so through a *symbol*. The symbol, for Jung, is the best possible expression of something which is basically unknown. It is a libido analogue, a transformer of energy. It transforms energy in the unconscious into an equivalent conscious form. The symbol is not consciously created but is a spontaneous formation out of the unconscious. This "image" comes forth pregnant with meaning. It provides partial understanding but, as symbol, it points to what cannot be understood.

Images, whether within the psyche or outside in the environment, become symbols when they give a specific content to an archetype. The image then becomes a route to the energy of the archetype, making that energy available for the development of consciousness and the growth of the personality as a whole.

For example, the archetype of the self appears in dreams, myths, fairytales, and the imagination through images such as king, savior, prophet, or in the form of a circle, square, or cross. The mandala, such as Teresa's castle, is one of the symbols of the self.

Jung pointed to the cross as a clear example of a symbol. When the cross is explained as a representation of divine love, then it is a sign merely pointing to its explanation in the words "divine love." But when the cross is symbolic it is pointing to depths of experience which cannot be communicated in another way. When the cross is symbolic it is experienced as the point of contact with divine mystery.

Whether or not an image is symbolic depends upon two considerations. In the first place, an image becomes a symbol

when the person observing the image is open to symbolic inter-
pretations. The observer must have an attitude which allows the
image to express something unknown. Consequently, an image
may be symbolic to one person but not to another. On the other
hand, certain images are symbolic simply by the effect they have
on observers. They immediately conjure up symbolic interpre-
tations.[15]

The above definitions and descriptions are a partial presentation of Jung's psychology. These terms generally relate to the
nature and structure of the psyche. Other aspects of his psychology will be presented in later chapters. In particular, the next
chapter will discuss the unfolding and development of personality which Jung called the Individuation Process.

Teresa and the Psyche

It is apparent that Teresa is writing about a religious journey through the castle which is, at the same time, a story of the
psyche. Her image of water is an image of human interiority.
Her assumption is that religious growth is accompanied by psychological growth. Knowledge of God requires knowledge of
self. As a matter of fact she encourages people to linger in the
room of self-knowledge in the castle. She writes: "For never,
however exalted the soul may be, is anything else more fitting
than self-knowledge. . . . Without it everything goes wrong. . . .
Knowing ourselves is something so important that I wouldn't
want any relaxation ever in this regard, however high you may
have climbed into the heavens. . . . Let's strive to make more
progress in self-knowledge, for in my opinion we shall never
completely know ourselves if we don't strive to know God."[16]

We realize that religious development and psychological development do not necessarily go hand-in-hand. Individuals who
are psychologically maladjusted may respond quite heroically to
God in their lives. Certainly psychological health is a relative
matter. Severely limited personalities remind us that our salvation does not depend upon our mental health or mental capacities. Life itself and the varying abilities to respond to life are all
gift from God. However, all things being equal, a deepening

union with God generally is accompanied by a more integrated personality and a greater focus of energy in God's service. Although she lacks adequate psychological categories, Teresa reminds us that we do not go to God by losing ourselves, but by finding ourselves. She stresses the need for humility which is another way of saying that we must be anchored in reality. This reality requires a knowledge, and acceptance, of ourselves.

In *The Interior Castle* Teresa is entering more deeply into the psyche, into the unconscious part of the psyche. It is not an entirely voluntary movement because she is called by the unconscious, just as she was attracted by water. She enters within and descends. Spatial references such as "within" used by Teresa and "down" used in depth psychology are not meant to be actual locations. But they are metaphors used naturally by human consciousness and they have a tradition in spiritual and psychological literature.

Teresa experienced the transpersonal layer of the psyche, the layer Jung called the collective unconscious. Her pilgrimage involved experiencing the polarities of the psyche as they sought equilibrium. These polarities become part of the great polarity moving toward reconciliation in the castle, the polarity of the human and divine, of Teresa and God. Jung called the collective unconscious the objective psyche since that realm is as objective and "other" as is the outer cosmos. And while he does not identify the collective unconscious with God, it is the medium for contact with God, the point of openness to that which is beyond us yet met within us.

According to Jung's theory, the archetypes in the objective psyche prefigured Teresa's development. Archetypal patternings disposed her to experiences which allowed the self to emerge. But since the archetypes are not known directly, Teresa needed symbols to lead her to them. Key images in *The Interior Castle* both led her into depth experiences and, at the same time, were vehicles for transforming archetypal energy and making it available for Teresa's self-realization. These images, then, in a very real way not only tell her story but *are* her story. They are living images, pregnant with meaning.

Such a literal application of Jungian psychology to the experiences and writing of Teresa is not meant to be a claim of total understanding. Jung never claimed his theories to be a definitive statement concerning the psyche. All that he could claim was that the psyche acted "as if." A Jungian reading of *The Interior Castle* is an attempt to gain understanding by viewing the castle story "as if."

Certainly the images in the castle give every evidence for meeting Jung's criteria for a symbol. Certain images, such as the castle, seem to be spontaneous formations of the unconscious. Other images, such as water, appear symbolic because of the effect they have on Teresa. And still other images are symbolic because of Teresa's attitude. Her observing consciousness is open to symbolic interpretation: "I believe that in each little thing created by God there is more than what is understood, even if it is a little ant."[17]

The symbol of water has led us into this discussion of the psyche, particularly the unconscious and its riches. Carl Jung's categories have provided an orientation to this inner realm. He echoes Teresa in urging an inner journey. His view of the psyche offers a hope of finding purpose and direction through a descent into the unconscious. And he demonstrates the necessity of living a symbolic life if the psyche is to express itself and develop.

The seventh dwelling place represents the final manifestation and union of the self and God. Here, too, Teresa offers water as symbolic of the experience of union: "In the spiritual marriage the union is like what we have when rain falls from the sky into a river or fount; all is water, for the rain that fell from heaven cannot be divided or separated from the water of the river. Or it is like what we have when a little stream enters the sea: there is no means of separating the two."[18]

Concluding Reflections and Suggestions

Jung stated that contemporary people have lost their souls. As the level of consciousness rises, greater individuality is possible, and so is greater restlessness. Psychology did not cause today's psychic problems. The growing psychic needs produced the environment for the development of a science of the psyche. Depth psychology is a response to contemporary loss of soul.

People who live with a collective mentality keep in touch with their roots through the symbols and rites of the culture. The individual who steps out of the container of the collective with a developing consciousness risks losing touch with the roots. Without collective symbols to provide identity and meaning, a person is left to wrestle alone with inner forces. The forces are no longer channeled by the community to which one belonged.

In becoming more conscious, Jung believes, modern people have simultaneously discarded that which would give meaning. In losing contact with their roots they have lost their souls, lost themselves. Jung sees the solution lying in the unconscious, but means are not readily available for contacting the unconscious.

The churches were previously able to bridge the gap between the unconscious and consciousness. Psychic energies found an outlet in the symbols of religion. While these channels remained open we were able to meet ourselves in these outward expressions. There was no need for an inner journey. The psyche was carried for us by an outer container, the church. But once the symbols of religion no longer expressed our personal experiences, once the channels were blocked-up and the psyche began to flow back upon itself, then the psyche became a factor in its own right.

In a rational, technical, too-conscious age, the symbols of religion lose their power to enhance the development of the self. A regression of energies takes place and the psyche becomes a source of disintegration rather than wholeness. At least, so runs Carl Jung's analysis of our contemporary situation. My own experience leads me to believe that Jung is accurate in his analysis.

The way back to meaning is suggested in Jung's description of religion. "Religion appears to me," he wrote, "to be a peculiar attitude of mind which could be formulated in accordance with the original use of the word *religio*, which means a careful consideration and observation of certain dynamic factors that are conceived as 'powers': spirits, daemons, gods, laws, ideas, ideals, or whatever name man has given to such factors in his world as he has found powerful, dangerous, or helpful enough to be taken into careful consideration, or grand, beautiful, and meaningful enough to be devoutly worshipped and loved."[19]

Religion is an attitude of mind characterized by a thoughtful, reflective consideration of numinous experience. Numinous experience, manifested through the unconscious, exerts an irresistible power which both attracts and repels since it is experienced as something far greater than the person herself.

Religion as creed is a containment for this primordial experience. The rituals and symbols, including the dogmas, express and channel primordial experience and at the same time open people to their numinous moments. Religion as creed maintains a balance which is well articulated by Ann and Barry Ulanov in *Religion and the Unconscious:*

> The first balance that religion provides is to safeguard human sanity by presenting a context of tradition and dogma, records of experiences of the divine in which to contain and observe the fierce brightness of our own revelation. Conversely, these individual experiences feed into religious tradition, making it a living, contemporary configuration of the truth of religious mystery. The transcendent has become immanent, not by a process of reasoning, but through the immediacy of experience.[20]

A danger, Jung warned, is that religion as creed loses touch with the immediacy of experience. Codified and dogmatized forms of original religious experience tend to become rigid, elaborately structured ideas which tend to conceal experience. When this occurs, religion becomes an activity totally outside personal experience. Religion no longer points to the presence of God in my experiences. It is a world in itself, drawing me out of my own world and away from a nourishing contact with God in my depths. The symbols of religion then dry up. As one woman said to me, "One day in the middle of Mass I said to myself, 'There is nothing here for me.' And I got up and left, and have never returned."

A serious challenge for the Christian churches, I believe, is to help people find the paschal mystery in their own lives. In other words, where in my life am I experiencing the dying and rising of Christ? When I can find the sacred places in my life where God contacts me then I can celebrate that life in church. But in order to hear God in my life I have to be aware of my symbols which express that experience. My symbols may not look like someone else's symbols. I will have my own symbolic expressions for my brokenness, my experience of healing, my dyings and risings. My symbols then begin to flesh-out the Christian symbols, and the Christian symbols then challenge and contextualize my symbols within the Christian community. Again, I need to learn to tell my story, in order to better hear and be nourished by the Christian story.

Today, numerous religious education programs attempt to relate the Christian teachings to people's experience. Both the community story and the individual story are being heard. One example of such a catechetical approach is a process which Thomas Groome calls "shared praxis."[21] Groome has used this process in a variety of settings, including classrooms, retreats, and adult education programs.

In this process, first of all, a topic is agreed upon. Let us say it is the issue of divorce. Each person in the group then reflects upon that topic out of his or her own experience. This story is quietly listened to by the rest of the group. It is not a time of criticism or correction.

Once each person has had sufficient time to speak to the issue of divorce from his or her history and point of view, then the Christian tradition regarding divorce is presented. The tradition is presented as accurately and completely as possible. It too is given a careful hearing by the group.

Now, both stories are present: the individual's and the Christian community's. The next step is to have the group reflect upon the meaning of each story for the other story. Does the story of the Christian community provide a context, a new perspective for the individual story? Does the individual story affirm, deny, or point beyond the present understanding of the

Christian tradition? Each story asserts itself against the other story and each is critiqued by the other.

This dialectic leads to a final step in the process. In this step the individual and the group are moved to make some type of faith response in the light of the discussion that has just taken place. The response may be as simple as an intention to pursue the topic further. Or it may involve more demanding decisions. In this step the tradition of the past and the experience of the present are viewed in the context of the future and the demands of the kingdom of God. The faith response is an effort, in some way, to be creative of that future.

A similar process is used in the pastoral reflection seminars of the Washington Theological Union. In these seminars the men and women who are being prepared for ministry in the Catholic Church are asked to relate their experiences in ministry with the theology being learned in the classroom. The ministerial experience is fully and sensitively recounted. Patterns and themes emerge which require reflection. Sources from the theological tradition illumine the themes and patterns. A dialogue develops in which the experience of ministry and the theological tradition critique one another. They are compared and contrasted. Slowly, insights evolve and, along with them, possible implications for both theology and pastoral practice, as well as for personal faith.

What Carl Jung's theories bring to these processes is an understanding of the complexity involved in hearing one's experience, telling one's story. He warns that there is more to our meaning than our ego would have us believe. In our ministry we are meeting ourselves, the self, in a thousand different disguises. The self is expressing itself in the images resulting from our experience. Jung suggests ways of locating the images and allowing their meaning to become part of the story we are telling. The theological tradition, then, will have a worthy partner for the dialogue. The following chapters continue to present the depth-work of both Jung and Teresa.

Religion is obedience to awareness, said Jung. Teresa wrote, "... the gate of entry to this castle is prayer and reflection."[22] *The Interior Castle,* a document of both psyche and soul, relates the story that emerged as one Christian prayerfully attended to depth experiences.

NOTES

1. Jung, *Memories,* p. 7.
2. Jung, C.W., IXi, 40.
3. Ibid., IXi, 39.
4. Ibid., IXi, 40.
5. C.G. Jung, *Visions Seminars,* vol. 2, notes of Mary Foote (Zurich: Spring Publications, 1976), pp. 409, 410.
6. Lancelot L. Whyte, *The Unconscious Before Freud* (New York: Basic Books, Inc., 1960), p. 63.
7. From *Psyche: Zur Entwicklunsgeschichte der Seele* (1846). Quoted in Whyte, op. cit., p. 55.
8. *Interior Castle,* IV, chap. 2, no. 2
9. Ibid., IV, chap. 2, no. 3.
10. Ibid., IV, chap. 2, no. 4.
11. Ibid., VI, chap. 5, no. 3.
12. Ibid., IV, chap. 2, no. 5.
13. This distinction is discussed by Ann and Barry Ulanov in *Religion and the Unconscious* (Philadelphia: The Westminster Press, 1975), pp. 81ff.
14. Jung, C.W., IXi, 63. Volume VI of Jung's *Collected Works,* titled *Psychological Types,* contains definitions of his principal psychological concepts. Volume VII, *Two Essays on Analytical Psychology,* presents discussions of basic Jungian theory. Helpful, systematic presentations of Jung's theories are provided by: Jolande Jacobi, *The Psychology of C.G. Jung* (New Haven: Yale University Press, 1968); Ira Progoff, *Jung's Psychology and Its Social Meaning* (New York: Anchor Books, 1973); Calvin Hall and Vernon Nordby, *A Primer of Jungian Psychology* (New York: The New American Library, 1973).
15. When asked about procedures used in determining the existence of an archetype, Jung chose the figure of the prophet Elias as an example. Because the biography of Elias contains mythical elements and because posterity has added legends and parallels to Elias, "there is no longer any doubt we are dealing with an archetype." Jung details some of the traditions surrounding the prophet, finally concluding: "It is unnecessary to continue this long list of *phenomena of assimilation*

which follow without interruption, so to speak, from the remotest times to our own day. This proves irrefutably that Elijah is a *living archetype*. In psychology, we call it a *constellated archetype*, that is to say, one that is more or less generally active, giving birth to new forms of assimilation. One of these phenomena was the choice of Carmel for the foundation of the first convent in the twelfth century. The mountain had long been a numinous place as the seat of the Canaanite deities Baal and Astarte.... The numinous inhabitant of Carmel is chosen as the patron of the order. The choice is curious and unprecedented....

"I have already said that the archetype 'gets itself chosen' rather than is deliberately chosen. I prefer this way of putting it because it is almost the rule that one follows unconsciously the attraction and suggestion of the archetype. I think that the legend of Elijah and the unique atmosphere of Mount Carmel exercised an influence from which the founder of the order could no more withdraw himself than could the Druses, the Romans, Jews, Canaanites, or Phoenicians. It was not only the *place* which favoured the choice for the adoption of a compensatory figure but the *time*. The twelfth century and the beginning of the thirteenth were just the period which activated the spiritual movements brought into being by the new aeon which began with the eleventh century. These were the days of Joachim of Flora and the Brethren of the Free Spirit, of Albertus Magnus and Roger Bacon, of the beginning of Latin alchemy and of the natural sciences and also of a feminine religious symbol, the Holy Grail" (Jung, C.W., XVIII, 1519ff.).

More specifically, Jung theorized that the "probably historical" figure of Elias represents both the self and the collective unconscious in general. In the years when Jung was experimenting with confronting his unconscious, the figure of Elias presented itself to his imagination. Jung dialogued with Elias and learned that the unconscious has an autonomous life which can be met in a personification. The figure of Elias soon transformed into another figure whom Jung called Philemon. Jung wrote: "It was he who taught me psychic objectivity, the reality of the psyche. Through him the distinction was clarified between myself and the object of my thought. He confronted me in an objective manner, and I understood that there is something in me which can say things that I do not know and do not intend, things which may even be directed against me.... Psychologically, Philemon represented superior insight" (cf. Jung, *Memories*, pp. 181-3). Jung designated the figure represented by Elias and Philemon as the archetype of the wise old man.

16. *Interior Castle*, I, chap. 2, nos. 8, 9.

17. Ibid., IV, chap. 2, no. 2.

18. Ibid., VII, chap. 2, no. 4.

19. Jung, C.W., XI, 8.

20. Ulanov, op. cit., p. 36.

21. Thomas Groome, *Christian Religious Education* (San Francisco: Harper and Row, 1980), pp. 207–32.

22. *Interior Castle*, I, chap. 1, no. 7.

CHAPTER FOUR

A Map For Life's Journey

The fact that we change as we grow through life is evident. Just what the changes are all about is not so evident. Often they seem to be a series of random crises with no noticeable patterns or development involved. In some lives change is strikingly obvious; in other lives it can barely be detected.

But change we do. And modern developmental studies tell us that we can expect our lives to follow certain broad patterns as we move through our years. The theme of journey is an apt theme and image which reminds us that we are a people in process of becoming. As will be seen, Teresa of Avila was not unaware of our developmental nature.

Carl Jung's studies have been particularly helpful in mapping the development of the psyche. Jung identified this dynamic of the psyche as the underlying archetypal pattern which is expressed in the various hero stories of mythology. Just as the ego develops from the womb of the unconscious and later must re-enter the unconscious to reach the goal of the self, so the hero in mythology has a wonderful birth, journeys forth, and undergoes great testing to reach the goal.

Jung writes about the hero, and, presumably, heroines: "It is precisely the strongest and best among men, the heroes, who give way to their regressive longing and purposely expose themselves to the danger of being devoured by the monster of the maternal abyss. But if a man is a hero, he is a hero because, in the final reckoning, he did not let the monster devour him, but subdued it, not once but many times. Victory over the collective psyche alone yields the true value—the capture of the hoard, the invincible weapon, the magic talisman, or whatever it be that the myth deems most desirable. Anyone who identifies with the collective psyche—or, in mythological terms, lets himself be devoured by the monster—and vanishes in it, attains the treasure that the dragon guards, but he does so in spite of himself and to his own greatest harm."[1]

The libido of the psyche expresses itself in such a patterned way that it would be surprising if this patterning were not present in *The Interior Castle*. In discussing the extent of this pattern, Jung notes "the world-wide and pre-Christian motif of the hero and rescuer who, although devoured by the monster, appears again in a miraculous way, having overcome the dragon or whale or whatever it was that swallowed him. How, when, and where such a motif originated nobody knows. We do not even know how to set about investigating the problem in a sound way. Our only certainty is that every generation, so far as we can see, has found it as an old tradition. Thus we can safely assume that the motif 'originated' at a time when man did not yet know that he possessed a hero myth—in an age, therefore, when he did not yet reflect consciously on what he was saying. The hero figure is a typical image, an archetype, which has existed since time immemorial."[2]

Specifically, the hero myth represents the development of the psyche with the self as the goal. Jung called this development of the psyche the individuation process.

The Individuation Process: First Phase

The two main phases of the individuation process correspond to the first and second halves of life. The first half of life is characterized by expansion of the personality and adaptation to the outer world. The second half of life is characterized by a restriction or reduction which signifies an adaptation to the inner life. Schopenhauer said: "The first forty years of life furnish the text, while the remaining thirty supply the commentary;

without the commentary we are unable to understand aright the true sense and coherence of the text, together with the moral it contains."[3]

The transition from the first phase of the individuation process to the second phase is often a time of great difficulty and tension. The demands of life are different in the two phases and, consequently, the rules change. Learning the new rules may take time and be painful. Some people, of course, slip quietly from one phase to another. But it is also apparent that a broad maturity of personality comes to those whose mid-life transition has been a particularly difficult and challenging time. Their psyche has a unity and power which is the result of hard-earned development.

In saying that the phases of individuation correspond to the halves of life, Jung was expressing a general psychological truth. Individual personalities may develop according to a different schedule. The individuation process may be well advanced in a young person.[4] Inner and outer adaptations need to take place in both halves of life. Still, the first and second halves of life have a definite relationship to the two phases of individuation. This overall contour of life is helpful in understanding even the smaller outer and inner journeys which take place throughout life.

Giving impetus to both phases of the individuation process is the self. It is the objective of the process and at the same time the center of the process giving it dynamism. The self, as it were, calls the process into being and keeps it moving.

The first phase of the individuation process, corresponding to the first half of life, is an initiation into outer reality. It begins in the womb of all psychic life, the unconscious. In the beginning the individual is in a state of primal unity with all the opposites contained in the unconscious. Erich Neumann, a Jungian psychologist, has called this unity the "uroboric" state. The "uroborus" is an Egyptian symbol, a circular snake which is the primal dragon of the beginning. "It slays, weds, and impregnates itself. It is man and woman, begetting and conceiving, devouring and giving birth, active and passive, above and below, at once."[5] This symbol, a snake or dragon biting its own tail, represents a timeless unity, a psychic life prior to the emergence of any ego. This circle of unity appears at the beginning of the individuation process under the symbol of the primal deity, the serpent. It reappears as the goal of the individuation process under the symbol of the mandala. The Garden of Eden is a scriptural symbol representing the same psychic beginnings where all is in harmony.

Jung speaks of three stages of consciousness in the first half of life.[6] In the beginning, just glimmerings of consciousness arise from the all-embracing unconscious. This stage is an anarchic or chaotic state of consciousness. The individual merely perceives connections between two or more psychic contents, but there is no memory. Consciousness is sporadic. Jung likened it to islands which, in turn, he likened to tiny, twinkling lights in a far-flung darkness.

But these islands of memory begin to take on a continuity; an ego is developing. At first the ego is merely observed by the child, and the child will speak of itself objectively, in the third person. When the child speaks of itself in the first person it is an indication that the energy of the developing ego-complex is strong enough to give a sense of subjectivity or "I-ness." Jung called this developed ego-complex the monarchic or monistic state of consciousness. It consists, primarily, in a continuity of ego-memories.

Jung maintained that the child is not fully born until psychic birth has been completed at puberty. Puberty is the normal time of conscious differentiation from the parents. The parents have provided the safe, secure environment which has allowed the child to internalize a healthy sense of self. Upon that psychic foundation the ego begins its development. But until puberty, the child lives in the psychic atmosphere of the parents. It has no real personal problems because it cannot be at variance with itself.

At puberty the child moves out of the protective atmosphere into a problematic world of tensions. Tensions arise in the outer world as well as in the inner world. For the first time a person may be at variance with her own inner life. Competing impulses catch the ego in the middle. It is another step forward in consciousness which Jung calls the divided or dualistic state. This period of youth extends from just after puberty until middle life, which begins between the thirty-fifth and fortieth year.

The essential feature of this dualistic phase is a widening of the horizons of life and the inevitable resulting conflicts. At the same time that life seeks expansion, it is being resisted by something in the psyche which wants to remain in a childhood consciousness. The unconscious exerts a kind of inertia. Something in us wishes to remain unconscious or conscious only of the ego and not of any conflicting parts of the psyche.

But consciousness brings problems. The young person is aware of inner expectations and outer limitations. False assumptions about the world and one's place in it bring about confusion. Inner psychic equilibrium is disturbed by inferiority feelings, tender sensitivities, and sexual impulses. Consciousness brings an awareness of opposites and their tensions. This state is imaged in Scripture as the condition east of Eden. And there is no going back to the garden. An angel guards the gate.

Jung writes with insight concerning the solution of the tensions in this first half of life. It is not a time for a balancing of the opposites in order to have a whole personality. This is left for later in life. Jung writes that "society does not value these feats of the psyche very highly; its prizes are always given for achievement and not for personality, the latter being rewarded for the most part posthumously. These facts compel us towards a particular solution: we are forced to limit ourselves to the attainable, and to differentiate particular aptitudes in which the socially effective individual discovers his true self."[7] In order to adapt to the outer world certain tasks must be accomplished as ego-consciousness develops.

One of the tasks in the first half of life or in the first phase of the individuation process is the establishment of a *persona*. A persona is a mask, or a number of masks, through which the individual relates to the world around. Masks are a means of adaptation to society and a protection for the psyche. A raw psyche, without the mediation of a persona, would be a jarring experience for the individual as well as society. And it would be an unhealthy situation.

There are conditions, however, which determine whether a mask is healthy or not. A mask has to be a sensitive balance of a number of ingredients. First of all, a healthy mask is composed of expectations I have for myself. The persona I wear embodies, to some degree, the view I have of myself, my hopes, my ideals. I have different masks for different occasions, and, consequently, different views of myself are highlighted. For example, a businessman will have a different persona at work from the one he shows at home with his family.

A second consideration in the composition of a healthy persona is the expectations of others. If I am to expand into the world around me, if I am to fit in and be effective and accepted, my persona must not be a total surprise or disappointment to others. Others have legitimate expectations of me as I take my place in the adult world, and these expectations help shape my persona. A certain professional, competent demeanor is expected of a physician, and rightly so. Whether he feels professional on a given day or wants to act with the appropriate seriousness is irrelevant. People want continuity and reliability in another's persona. We learn how to enter into life and adapt to the world through the shaping of others.

A third ingredient of a healthy mask or persona is the reality of my personality. My very real possibilities as a developing individual condition the formation of a healthy persona. I cannot pretend to be something I am not, especially when the pretense causes me to lose touch with my real personality and saps the energy I need to continue to grow. Unless my expectations of myself and others' expectations of me are grounded in the realities of my personality, my persona becomes unbalanced. I begin to be caught up in my persona, and to identify totally with my roles in life.

The businessman who is also the businessman at home, and only a businessman, loses touch with parts of himself. The doctor who must, in every situation, be recognized as a healer never has an opportunity to face his own sicknesses. The mother who is totally identified with that role to the extent that she recognizes no other needs, possibilities, or limitations must deny unmotherly feelings and responses if she is to be at peace with herself. The priest who compresses his personality into that persona to the extent that he cannot admit aggressive feelings or selfish desires begins to drain that personality of life. In totally living out my own expectations or others' expectations I build a life that rests on extremely fragile foundations. Too easily it can tumble down. The whole life structure can become unwieldly and actually unlivable.

But a healthy persona has a certain vitality and flexibility. It is an acknowledgement that I must be responsible and dependable in relating to various situations in life. At the same time it demonstrates that I am not neglecting my inner life and the ongoing relationship with that world which must be nurtured.

A persona develops as other tasks are accomplished in the first phase of the individuation process. These tasks are integral to the persona. One of the tasks is the development of a main attitude in life, either extroversion or introversion. The other task is the development of a predominant function from among the four psychological functions of thinking, feeling, intuiting, and sensing. The two attitudes and four functions were described in the last chapter.

Because the psyche contains polarities of energy, and because these polarities, by definition, are opposites, they cannot be developed at the same time. The two attitudes and four functions are ways of naming some of the polarities of the psyche. In the first half of life it becomes important, and realistic, to develop one side of these polarities. Increasing consciousness means increasing differentiation. Only one pole at a time can be integrated into the conscious personality and begin to give a particular shape to that personality.

Extroversion or introversion will be a dominant attitude in the first half of the individuation process. Heredity begins this determination, and life-experiences enhance it. One of the perceiving functions, sensation or intuition, will be developed; the other will not. And only one of the judging functions will be developed, thinking or feeling.

Now each polarity is actually a continuum and, in reality, both attitudes and all four functions will have some role to play in an individual's conscious personality. But, in general, certain poles will be better integrated in consciousness than their opposites. These opposites, for the most part, continue to reside in the unconscious. If there is not a differentiation and development of specific poles of personality, the individual does not adapt well to the outer environment. The person may appear either unpredictable and childish, or rigid in an attempt to cover up a lack of differentiation.

The emergence of an extroverted attitude or introverted attitude is a primary task of the first half of life. Whichever pole is not integrated into conscious living becomes a fixture of the unconscious and is something to be met in time. To identify with one or the other pole is a necessary risk for ego-development.

Each pole has consequences which are perceived as negative. Obviously, since the extrovert's energy flows outward toward the environment, his adaptation to the outer world is often less troubled than is the introvert's adaptation. In the second stage of the individuation process or the second half of life, the introvert may look back and feel that he has missed out on a good part of life.

On the other hand, the introvert is usually more at home with the inner journey of the second phase of the individuation process than is the extrovert. The extrovert facing the second half of life may feel that he has dried up inside and there is no life within him. Each needs to contact the neglected attitude-pole.

The emergence of a predominant function becomes another primary task of the first half of life. While one of the perceiving functions and one of the judging functions will be integrated into the conscious personality, usually one of these functions predominates. One function becomes the primary way that the psyche assimilates material coming from without and within. One person may predominantly use a thinking function in all situations. Another continually responds from an intuitive standpoint. We each generally rely on one basic "mode of apprehension" in relating to life. That function becomes the best developed of the four functions.

The second best developed function is called the auxiliary

function. If the predominant function is a judging function, then the auxiliary function is one of the perceiving functions, and vice versa. In other words, we will have one fairly well developed way of taking in our experiences, and one fairly well developed manner of judging them. The predominant function and the auxiliary function are both well-established parts of the conscious personality.

The function opposite the predominant function resides deepest in the unconscious and is called the inferior function. For example, if intuition is my predominant function, then its polar opposite, sensation, is my inferior function. As the function deepest in the unconscious, the inferior function is the weakest function, the least developed, and a possible negative source. The recovery of the inferior function becomes one of the tasks in the second phase of the individuation process.

But in the first phase, I need to acknowledge and integrate one perceiving and one judging function. These functions and my main attitude add to the particular cast of my persona.

The result of the first phase of the individuation process must be a strong ego-consciousness with a well developed persona. Without this result, the second phase of the individuation process cannot begin. Someone who has not successfully accomplished the outer journey is not ready for the inner journey. Often people will arrive at the second half of their lives without a comfortable persona or a healthy ego. In this situation contact with the unconscious has to wait until consciousness can be shored up.

While Jungian theory generally discourages an identification of the ego with the persona, often today efforts must be made to strengthen the persona. Without a good rooting in the outer world and a healthy identity, the psychic conditions are not present for the second phase of the individuation process which presumes a firm base in consciousness for the entry into the unconscious.

In the first half of life a certain one-sidedness is called for. It is not a time for a rounded personality. A certain amount of unreflective activity and spontaneity is beneficial in a person moving out into the world. The dilemmas created by a full psychic birth at puberty find a temporary resolution as the individual attempts to fit into society. In fitting into society all other psychic possibilities have to be renounced. As Jung writes, "One man loses a valuable piece of his past, another a valuable piece of his future. Everyone can call to mind friends or schoolmates who were promising and idealistic youngsters, but who, when we meet them again years later, seem to have grown dry and cramped in a narrow mould.... The serious problems in life, however, are never fully solved. If ever they should appear to be so it is a sure sign that something has been lost. The meaning and purpose of a problem seem to lie not in its solution but in our working at it incessantly. This alone preserves us from stultification and petrifaction."[8]

The temporary solution of the first half of life does lie in a certain petrifaction. The ego becomes entrenched in one's personality. Toward the end of the first phase of the individuation process the position of the ego as a firm center of consciousness becomes consolidated. But it is only a temporary solution.

The situation is best described by Jung: "The nearer we approach to the middle of life, and the better we have succeeded in entrenching ourselves in our personal attitudes and social positions, the more it appears as if we had discovered the right course and the right ideals and principles of behaviour. For this reason we suppose them to be eternally valid, and make a virtue of unchangeably clinging to them. We overlook the essential fact that the social goal is attained only at the cost of a diminution of personality. Many—far too many—aspects of life which should also have been experienced lie in the lumber-room among dusty memories; but sometimes, too, they are glowing coals under grey ashes."[9]

The breakdown of the persona signals the beginning of the second phase of the individuation process. The development of the personality begins with consciousness emerging from the unconscious. The collective psyche is repressed so that the individual may develop. In forming a persona the individual takes on the collective consciousness of the community. He internalizes this consciousness with its attitudes, identity, and worldview. Jung believed that there was an excessive preponderance of the rational, extroverted persona in particular. In any case, the persona does not represent the full personality of the individual. It is highly vulnerable. In time, the persona can no longer contain the full personality which is seeking expression. The "glowing coals" buried deep in the personality begin to break into flames. An excessive commitment to the persona brings about a reaction in the unconscious. The persona begins to break down or disintegrate.

The Individuation Process: Second Phase

At this time in life, often about mid-life, the psyche spontaneously seeks equilibrium. As certain poles of personality are developed in consciousness, their opposites slowly become energized and they seek expression in the personality. The intensity of the energy in the unconscious begins to disrupt the apparently settled conscious life. The persona is shaken and the ego is decentered.

"The worst of it all," Jung writes, "is that intelligent and cultivated people live their lives without even knowing of the possibility of such transformations. Wholly unprepared, they embark upon the second half of life. Or are there perhaps colleges for forty-year-olds which prepare them for their coming life and its demands as the ordinary colleges introduce our young people to a knowledge of the world? No, thoroughly unprepared we take the step into the afternoon of life; worse still, we take this step with the false assumption that our truths and ideals will serve us as hitherto. But we cannot live the afternoon of life according to the programme of life's morning; for what was great in the morning will be little at evening, and what in the morning was true will at evening have become a lie. I have given psychological treatment to too many people of advancing years, and have looked too often into the secret chambers of their souls, not to be moved by this fundamental truth."[10]

The second phase of the individuation process generally coincides with this second half of life. This phase of the individuation process is the principal concern of Jungian psychology. At this time communication with the neglected unconscious begins in earnest. Individuation at this point in the development of personality refers to two processes or involves two meanings. On the one hand individuation refers to a process of psychic differentiation. The unconscious is attended to so that the neglected poles of the psyche may be recognized as having an autonomous existence in the unconscious. This differentiation process means that the individual comes to meet all the persons of the inner world which, together, are part of the self. Once these parts of the psyche have been brought to awareness and their independent identity has been recognized, then the second meaning of individuation is a possibility. This meaning refers to the state of being undivided. Consciousness and the unconscious are now in communication and parts of the self which are seeking expression in conscious living are now being recognized and integrated. This undivided state of the psyche allows for the development of a unique personality. Individuation, writes Jung, "is the process by which individual beings are formed and differentiated; in particular, it is the development of the psychological *individual* as a being distinct from the general, collective psychology. Individuation, therefore, is a process of *differentiation* having for its goal the development of the individual personality."[11]

Whereas the first phase of the individuation process is an outer journey to adapt to the collective, the second phase is an inner journey which carries one into the personal and collective layers of the unconscious. A firm base in consciousness is necessary because the purpose of the descent into the unconscious is to return to conscious living with more of one's self expressed in the conscious personality. Another way of speaking about the descent into the unconscious is the living of the symbolic life. The individuation process requires that I listen to my depths, and those depths are experienced through their symbolic expressions in my life. The ways of listening to inner images which were discussed in the first chapter, namely through feelings, projections, dreams and the process of active imagination, become routes to the unconscious layers of the psyche.

In his experiments with the inner journey through the images of the psyche, Jung identified certain archetypes or inner personalities which people will experience in the individuation process. These figures will be discussed in later chapters.

Individuation Within the Castle

The life of prayer is experienced as a journey. Teresa's image of journey, of movement through the castle, is so basic to her writing that it might be overlooked. And yet, upon reflection, journey is a major theme. It gives the reader a sense of narrative, of unfolding and development. Teresa writes of being on a path.[12] In other words, the soul is going somewhere. There is a destination to look forward to, and there is a way to that destination. A path has a certain configuration which, in time, will bring the traveler to its end.

On this path Teresa speaks of finding stages.[13] The journey has a rhythm of advances and rests, a pulse of its own. At each stage the terrain is different, and so too, then, are the experiences of the traveler. The differing stages of the journey evoke a variety of responses.

Teresa warns that the traveler walks a wearisome journey.[14] Arrival at the destination is not quick nor is it easy. This journey is accompanied by insecurities and difficulties, and requires a good amount of strength and courage. It would be presumptuous to undertake the journey without being invited, but the invitation, the necessity, is clear. "The journey I am speaking of," she writes, "must be taken with great humility."[15]

The movement through Teresa's inner castle has two phases. These phases correspond well to the two phases of the individuation process. The first phase involves the first three dwelling places. The second phase begins in the fourth dwelling place and continues through the remaining three dwelling places. The first three dwelling places are characterized by outer preoccupations, while the last three have a definite inner orientation. The first phase is active and controlling. The second phase is receptive and letting-go. The fourth dwelling place marks the transition from outer to inner and signals the deep interior work of the individuation process.

In the outer journey of the first phase a persona is continuing to develop and the ego is being strengthened. In terms of the life-cycle the first three dwelling places could reflect the years from adolescence, where an initial conversion and choice of vocation usually take place, to the mid-life years where a "second conversion" is needed.

Teresa's description of an individual in the first dwelling place demonstrates how one-sided their development has been. "It is a shame," she writes, "and unfortunate that through our own fault we don't understand ourselves or know who we are."[16] The reason is that the outer journey has been all-consuming. "Thus there are souls so ill and so accustomed to being involved in external matters that there is no remedy, nor does it seem they can enter within themselves."[17]

But Teresa reminds us that this individual in the first dwelling place has at least entered the outer rooms, and it is a beginning. She says: "For even though they are very involved in the world, they have good desires and sometimes, though only once in a while, they entrust themselves to our Lord and reflect on who they are, although in a rather hurried fashion. During the period of a month they will sometimes pray, but their minds are then filled with business matters that ordinarily occupy them. They are so attached to these things that where their treasure lies their heart goes also."[18] She may as well have said that where their identity is, so is their center. At this point their identity and energy, and consequently their interest, are coming from a successful adaptation to the outer world with its demands. At the same time, a healthy ego has developed which will slowly hear the call to further individuation. In the first rooms of the castle the many centers in the outer world are stiff competition for the center within the castle. Teresa sympathizes with these people, observing that "they are prevented from seeing the beauty of the castle and from calming down; they have done quite a bit just by having entered."[19]

The first dwelling place is a time of conscious effort at prayer and reflection. Teresa encourages this activity by providing the image of the bee which "doesn't fail to leave the beehive and fly about gathering nectar from the flowers. So it is with the soul in the room of self-knowledge; let it believe me and fly sometimes to ponder the grandeur and majesty of its God."[20] Active prayer here requires decision and effort. Without this active effort to listen within, the outer collective consciousness will prevail. Teresa notes that the people in the first rooms "are still absorbed in the world and engulfed in their pleasures and vanities, with their honors and pretenses. . . ."[21] In other words, these people are still identified with their persona. The preoccupations are a natural outcome of expansion into the world as the ego-consciousness develops from the unconscious. Teresa sums up the situation this way: "Even though it may not be in a bad state, it is so involved in worldly things and so absorbed with its possessions, honor, or business affairs, as I have said, that even though as a matter of fact it would want to see and enjoy its beauty these things do not allow it to; nor does it seem that it can slip free from so many impediments."[22]

The second dwelling place is a more demanding situation for the individual. "These rooms, in part," Teresa writes, "involve much more effort than do the first. . . ."[23] The second dwelling place calls for a steadier commitment to prayer. The individual has traveled closer to the center of the castle and the attraction from the center is now perceived as a personal call from God. The call from God begins to make demands on the individual who now is invited to make a personal response. Teresa wryly comments that "hearing His voice is a greater trial than not hearing it."[24] At this point the call from God is mediated through sermons, books, and people and events in one's life. In time, the center calls more clearly and directly.

Carl Jung spoke of the individuation process as a vocation. "True personality," he wrote, "is always a vocation and puts its trust in it as in God, despite its being, as the ordinary man would say, only a personal feeling. But vocation acts like a law of God from which there is no escape. The fact that many a man who goes his own way ends in ruin means nothing to one who has a vocation. He *must* obey his own law, as if it were a daemon whispering to him of new and wonderful paths. Anyone with a vocation hears the voice of the inner man: he is *called*."[25] There is an exigency to both the religious call and the psychological call, and Teresa located them in the one call coming from God who is center to a person's existence.

An active faith keeps the individual from retreating from this second dwelling place. Intellect, memory, and will combine to reinforce trust in the call that is being heard and the direction which is pointed out. Teresa, the psychologist, alertly diagnoses the problem that develops when the outer journey in life becomes a preoccupation: the inner life begins to call for attention. "Can there be an evil greater than that of being ill at ease in our own house?" she asks. "What hope can we have of finding rest outside of ourselves if we cannot be at rest within?"[26] One solution would be to ignore the inner life and redouble efforts to find security in the container of the collective. To live in the collective consciousness as in a safe harbor is tempting when the road to individuation appears so demanding with so little satisfaction. Teresa knows that this solution will not be able to last. Jung warned that the wrong way as well as the right way will cost. Attention has to be paid to the deeper dimensions of the self. "Through the blood He shed for us," Teresa pleaded, "I ask those who have not begun to enter within themselves to do so; and those who have begun not to let the war make them turn back."[27]

If turning inward is a step toward the self, why would Teresa describe the experience as a "war"? The reason is that the ego, in the course of its normal development in the first phase of the individuation process, establishes itself as the center of consciousness but assumes that it is the center of the entire psyche. Since the unconscious is, by definition, that which is unknown to consciousness, the ego has no knowledge of a deeper and wider self which is the true center of the psyche. The individual has worked hard in the first half of life to gain an identity, a foothold in the world. Specific attitudes and functions are developed and appropriate masks are worn. But just when the picture seems complete, new pieces of data begin to arrive from the self and the picture starts to become fragmented. During the inward journey, the ego has to move off center stage so that the self may come to the fore. It is a painful process. As Jung writes, "the experience of the self is always a defeat for the ego."[28] If Jung can use the word "defeat" to describe the experience, Teresa is appropriately using the word "war" in her encouragement not to turn back. As an aid in this encounter with the self, Teresa offers two pieces of advice: ". . . you cannot begin to recollect yourselves by force but only by gentleness . . ." and, ". . . consult persons with experience."[29]

In the third dwelling place the tensions between the outer and inner journeys increase and eventually a critical point is reached. On the one hand, a person in the third dwelling place now has a regular prayer life and is leading a practically model, adult Christianity. On the other hand, ego-consciousness has gained an even firmer hold over the personality, and even this admirable religious life has become part of a persona. Teresa's description of the individual in this dwelling place hints at the ego-control: "They long not to offend His Majesty, even guarding themselves against venial sins; they are fond of doing penance and setting aside periods for recollection; they spend their time well, practicing works of charity toward their neighbors, and are very balanced in their use of speech and dress and in the governing of their household—those who have them. Certainly, this is a state to be desired."[30]

Teresa emphasizes the well-ordered lives of these people. In other words, surprises and unacceptable challenges are minimized. They are satisfied that they know the whole story. "It's useless to give them advice," Teresa writes, "for since they have engaged so long in the practice of virtue they think that they can teach others. . . ."[31] And again, "Have no fear that they will kill themselves, for their reason is still very much in control."[32]

For all the apparent surface harmony of these well-ordered lives, the underside is something else again. Teresa's analysis is insightful. She notes that after a while on this plateau, a deterioration sets in. A disquiet begins to undermine the certainties. These people experience a dryness in prayer. Small problems and defeats are magnified by their too-tender sensitivities. They are fearful of losing control, but they cannot help themselves. Nor, apparently, can anyone else help them. "In sum," says Teresa, "I have found neither a way of consoling nor a cure for

such persons other than to show them compassion in their af-
fliction—and, indeed, compassion is felt on seeing them subject
to so much misery—and not contradict their reasoning."[33]

But Teresa does have a cure. These people must leave the
third dwelling place and continue the journey to the center of
the castle. Staying where they are will only make matters worse.
Teresa is speaking from experience because not only has she observed others who remained at this stage for many years, but she
herself spent eighteen years in a similar condition. Although
people in this third dwelling place are leading good lives, they
have not actually allowed themselves to be decentered. A firm
base has been established in consciousness, but now it is time for
a serious inward journey which means a letting-go of the tight
hold on ego-consciousness in order to learn more about the self.
Teresa encourages abandoning this hold: "If humility is lacking,
we will remain here our whole life—and with a thousand afflic-
tions and miseries. For since we will not have abandoned ourselves, this state will be very laborious and burdensome. We
shall be walking while weighed down with this mud of our human misery, which is not so with those who ascend to the remaining rooms."[34]

The fourth dwelling place marks a clear transition on the
journey to the center of the castle. "One noticeably senses a gentle drawing inward," Teresa writes.[35] "The senses and exterior
things seem to be losing their hold because the soul is recovering
what it had lost."[36] This interiorizing is a response to a call and
requires a careful attention. The work cannot be forced. The
centering is a gradual process as ego-consciousness learns to listen to the self.

Initially, the prayer at this stage of the journey remains an
active prayer of meditation but it becomes characterized by a
rapid absorption in God which Teresa names the prayer of recollection. It is a centering prayer but the normal vocal and mental prayer may accompany it. "And without any effort or noise,"
she counsels, "the soul should strive to cut down the rambling
of the intellect—but not suspend either it or the mind."[37] This
prayer of recollection appears to be a mixture of conscious activity and, at the same time, a letting-go when the center calls. It is

an introductory prayer to the deeper prayer of the fourth dwelling place, the prayer of quiet.

In the prayer of quiet, ego activity is minimal. Teresa encourages letting the intellect go. There is an outer and inner stillness with a loving openness to God. It is a time of a healing contact with depths of the self, and the absorption in God brings peace to the soul. "The soul experiences deep feelings when it sees itself close to God. Nor does the experience last so long...."[38] This prayer of quiet is an introduction to an even deeper prayer, the contemplative prayer of union beginning in the fifth dwelling place.

In the fourth dwelling place Teresa presents a summary of the individual's situation up to this point. It sets the stage for the second phase of the individuation process which begins in this fourth dwelling place:

> They say that the soul enters within itself and, at other times, that it rises above itself. With such terminology I wouldn't know how to clarify anything. This is what's wrong with me: that I think you will understand by my way of explaining, while perhaps I'm the only one who will understand myself. Let us suppose that these senses and faculties (for I have already mentioned that these powers are the people of this castle, which is the image I have taken for my explanation) have gone outside and have walked for days and years with strangers—enemies of the well-being of the castle. Having seen their perdition they've already begun to approach the castle even though they may not manage to remain inside because the habit of doing so is difficult to acquire. But still they are not traitors, and they walk in the environs of the castle. Once the great King, who is in the center dwelling place of this castle, sees their good will, He desires in His wonderful mercy to bring them back to Him. Like a good shepherd, with a whistle so gentle that even they themselves almost fail to hear it, He makes them recognize His voice and stops them from going so far astray and brings them back to

their dwelling place. And this shepherd's whistle has such power that they abandon the exterior things in which they were estranged from Him and enter the castle.[39]

It is apparent in the fourth dwelling place that the inner journey has begun in earnest. The individual's persona-identification has cracked and ego-consciousness no longer has total control of the psyche. A new, more powerful center is emerging which calls attention to itself and demands a response.

Concluding Reflections and Suggestions

The image of journey through the castle led to a discussion of the development of personality which Jung called the individuation process. If that individuation process, in its general outline, is normative for the human psyche as the self emerges, then it is reasonable to assume that this same general outline would be apparent in Teresa's account of a soul finding self as it grows in union with God at the center. The journey through the castle indicates a compatibility with the individuation process. The religious journey and the psychological journey are evidently one journey in Teresa's experience.

Carl Jung, too, could not separate the two developments: "Among all my patients in the second half of life—that is to say, over thirty-five—there has not been one whose problem in the last resort was not that of finding a religious outlook on life. It is safe to say that every one of them fell ill because he had lost what the living religions of every age have given to their followers, and none of them has been really healed who did not regain his religious outlook."[40]

In Jung's estimation, religion should be the school for forty-year-olds. He believed that the journey of the psyche through the individuation process is almost perfectly expressed in the dogmatic truths of the Christian Church. The self is the psychological equivalent of the kingdom of heaven which is within. The self is not God, but symbols for the self are indistinguishable from symbols for God. The experience of the self is as indescribable for Jung as union with God is for Teresa.

Jung writes: "At this point, unpalatable as it is to the scientific temperament, the idea of mystery forces itself upon the mind of the inquirer, not as a cloak for ignorance but as an admission of his inability to translate what he knows into the everyday speech of the intellect. I must therefore content myself with a bare mention of the archetype which is inwardly experienced at this stage, namely the birth of the 'divine child' or—in the language of the mystics—the inner man."[41]

The individuation process is not a narcissistic trip. It is actually a journey into community. Ego-consciousness is actually the isolated existence as it struggles for identity and control. Movement toward the self is a movement into a common life. The deeper down the psyche I descend, the less I am "I" and the more I am "we." We are each like a well that has its source in a common underground stream which supplies all. The deeper down the well I go, the closer I come to the source which puts me in contact with all other life.

An example of the individuation process leading to richer communal living can be seen in the use which is made of Jung's personality types. Arriving at one's own personality type takes a little effort and guesswork. Other people can be invaluable in helping us determine our type. And psychological instruments, such as the *Myers-Briggs Type Indicator*, can be the most helpful of all. I have frequently used that particular instrument in classes and workshops since it reveals the personality profile of an individual according to the categories of Jungian typology.

Once I have some understanding of my personality type I can more carefully own and respect the strengths I possess. My introversion may be seen in its positive aspects. My intuition and feeling functions are relied upon for their perceptiveness and accuracy.

Once I have an indication of my strengths, my preferences, I then can be more aware of the neglected poles of my personality. Because my extroversion, my thinking and sensing, may all be poorly developed, I may find myself defensive and touchy about these areas of my personality. And I may project my poorly developed attitude and functions upon someone who is actually quite strong in these areas. I will be critical or mistrustful of that person needlessly.

For example, someone with a poorly developed thinking function may view a thinking-type as a person who is "all up in his head." Similarly, a person with a poorly developed feeling function may judge another as a "bleeding heart" when actually that person has a well-integrated feeling function. When we become aware of our poorly developed functions we then are more alert to our projections and can withdraw them.

An understanding of my personality type helps me respect differing personalities. I am forewarned of the types I will not automatically understand. I am also alerted to the types of personalities which complement mine and whose viewpoint I need for a balanced perspective. Pastoral teams learn to cherish a variety of personalities because each brings a different perspective to ministry.

But we do not just rely on others to complement us. They represent poles of personality which I can slowly integrate into my conscious personality in my individuation process. Together we help one another grow into the deeper, wider life to which we are called.

Jung writes: "As nobody can become aware of his individuality unless he is closely and responsibly related to his fellow beings, he is not withdrawing to an egoistic desert when he tries to find himself. He can only discover himself when he is deeply and unconditionally related to some, and generally related to a great many, individuals with whom he has a chance to compare and from whom he is able to discriminate himself."[42]

And, again:

Individuation has two principal aspects: in the first place it is an internal and subjective process of integration, and in the second it is an equally indispensable process of objective relationship. Neither can exist without the other, although sometimes the one and sometimes the other predominates. This double aspect has two corresponding dangers. The first is the danger of the patient's using the opportunities for spiritual development arising out of the analysis of the unconscious as a pretext for evading the deeper human responsibilities, and for affecting a certain "spirituality" which cannot stand up to moral criticism; the second is the danger that atavistic tendencies may gain the ascendency and drag the relationship down to a primitive level. Between this Scylla and that Charybdis there is a narrow passage, and both medieval Christian mysticism and alchemy have contributed much to its discovery.[43]

Service in the world is the outcome of the journey through Teresa's castle. The quality of service of our brothers and sisters becomes Teresa's test of the reality of union with God. As the soul approaches the center, service becomes less mixed with ego needs and more open to God's view of the world and its needs. "This is the reason for prayer, my daughters, the purpose of this spiritual marriage: the birth always of good works, good works."[44]

The individuation process should take place within a community for a community. It is a sad realization to think about the number of people who undergo transformations alone. Our development is a precarious journey as it is, without the additional problem of having no companions on the journey. The transitions of the individuation process should be celebrated by the symbols and rituals of the Church, a community of people who are behind, alongside of, and ahead of me as I travel. The symbols invite me to enter necessary dyings as ego meets the self. I am supported in the descent into the unconscious by this community and its symbols point the way up to new life. The self begins to emerge and new commitments are made to the life of the community. Contact with the self puts me in touch with the wider community of brothers and sisters who minister to one another on the road to God's kingdom.

An example of a program which successfully incorporates the journey of an individual into the life of a faith community is the *Rite of Christian Initiation of Adults* in the Catholic Church. Individuals who are to be initiated into the Church are gradually introduced into the life and worship of the community. With the aid of catechists and sponsors these individuals share the stories of their lives and in turn learn about the life of the community they are joining. With the prayers, example, and fellowship of the community they discern in their lives God's call and consider their response. Slowly through the seasons of the liturgical year the stories of the individual and the community are intertwined in classes, worship, and service. Lent is an especially intense time, a final preparation for the sacraments of initiation at Easter. The individuals look at their stories through the Jesus story to find where and how in their lives they are being led to transformation, to conversion.

The significant point for our present concern is the fact that these adults are not undergoing transformation alone. The changes in their lives are being heard by a supporting group. The community of the Church challenges the adults to see in their crises and passages invitations to religious conversion. The symbols and liturgy celebrate this journey to God. Here the individuation process can take place in the midst of a faith community where the radical, God-oriented nature of this process can be affirmed.

While the rite is structured for the initiation of adults into the Church, the process it employs is recommended for all groups of Christians who are serious about their growth in faith. The process is one approach to the critical task of helping people relate the sacred figures of religion to their psyche. It is this relationship which is maintained in *The Interior Castle*.

The fourth dwelling place marks a major transition in life, the beginning of the inner journey, the second phase of the individuation process. The remaining dwelling places recount the experiences of one who is growing in union with God and approaching the deepest self. But this initial entry into the depths brings one face to face with dark forces. "I have greatly enlarged on this dwelling place," Teresa writes, "because it is the one that more souls enter. Since it is, and since the natural and the supernatural are joined in it, the devil can do more harm."[45]

The devils and their agents, the serpents, are the next images to be explored in the context of Jung's psychology.

NOTES

1. Jung, C.W., VII, 261. For further discussion about the hero myth cf.: Jung, C.W., V, 251ff; Joseph Campbell, *The Hero with a Thousand Faces* (Princeton University Press, 1968).

2. Jung, C.W., XVIII, 530.

3. Quoted in Jolande Jacobi, *The Way of Individuation* (New York: Harcourt, Brace, and World, Inc., 1967), p. 16.

4. Adolf Guggenbühl-Craig, a noted Jungian analyst, comments: "Jung's writings sometimes indicate that individuation takes place in the second half of life. Jung did not maintain the point dogmatically....

... In my analytical experience I have found that the individuation process may appear at *any* stage of life. I have often been able to observe it in young people, many of whom wrestle with the problems of God, death and the Devil. Such young people are completely open to the overall polarity of human existence, without being broken by it. They penetrate psychologically to the very depths of the nature of man and Creation. I have recognized in the dreams of such adolescents the symbols of individuation and the finding of the Self, and I have seen how they confront and are influenced by these symbols....

... An approach to the Self can take place at any age: a 16-year-old may be quite far along the path of individuation, while a 60-year-old may have completely abandoned the search. Throughout our lives we draw nearer to the center of our being, only to fall back from it again" (*Power in the Helping Professions*, pp. 139–141).

5. Erich Neumann, *The Origins and History of Consciousness* (Princeton University Press, 1954), p. 10.

6. Jung, C.W., VIII, 749ff. This essay, "The Stages of Life," provides an introductory framework.

7. Ibid., par. 768.

8. Ibid., pars. 770, 771.

9. Ibid., par. 772.

10. Ibid., par. 784.

11. Ibid., VI, 757.

12. *Interior Castle*, III, chap. 1, no. 1.

13. Ibid., IV, chap. 1, no. 3.
14. Ibid., III, chap. 2, no. 7.
15. Ibid., III, chap. 2, no. 8.
16. Ibid., I, chap. 1, no. 2.
17. Ibid., I, chap. 1, no. 6.
18. Ibid., I, chap. 1, no. 8.
19. Ibid.
20. Ibid., I, chap. 2, no. 8.
21. Ibid., I, chap. 2, no.12.
22. Ibid., I, chap. 2, no. 14.
23. Ibid., II, chap. 1, no. 2.
24. Ibid.
25. Jung, C.W., XVII, 300.
26. *Interior Castle*, II, chap. 1, no. 9.
27. Ibid.
28. Jung, C.W., XIV, 778.
29. *Interior Castle*, II, chap. 1, no. 10.
30. Ibid., III, chap. 1, no. 5.
31. Ibid., III, chap. 2, no. 1.
32. Ibid., III, chap. 2, no. 7.
33. Ibid., III, chap. 2, no. 2.
34. Ibid., III, chap. 2, no. 9.
35. Ibid., IV, chap. 3, no. 3.
36. Ibid., IV, chap. 3, no. 1.
37. Ibid., IV, chap. 3, no. 7.
38. Ibid., IV, chap. 3, no. 12.
39. Ibid., IV, chap. 3, no. 2.
40. Jung, C.W., XI, 509.
41. Jung, C.W., XVI, 482.
42. *C.G. Jung: Letters*, vol. 2, p. 592.
43. Jung, C.W., XVI, 448.
44. *Interior Castle*, VII, chap. 4, no. 6.
45. Ibid., IV, chap. 3, no. 13.

CHAPTER FIVE

Serpents and Devils in the Shadows

The inner journey phase of the individuation process puts us in touch with the neglected figures of our unconscious. And the first figure met on the journey is usually our *shadow*, a term used by Jung for the neglected, negative side of our personality.

I had always wondered why saintly people continually wrote about their sinfulness when it seemed to me that they were models of goodness. The reason for their sensitivity to the dark side of their lives is, I now believe, the fact that they were truly on an inner journey and were impressed with the experience of their brokenness and need for healing.

We cannot escape meeting the dark forces in us, and soon, when we set out to encounter the figures of our inner world. Not only is there a negative side of our personality residing in the shadow figure, but the entire realm of the collective unconscious has potentially destructive power and requires a cautious approach. Anyone whose ego consciousness, for a period of time, has been overwhelmed by unconscious forces can vouch for the powers within us.

Serpents and devils are typical images for the dark side of our psyche. *The Interior Castle* employs both images. In this chapter I will first present Teresa of Avila's use of the imagery, and then explore the images further through Jung's psychology. Together they lead us into a disturbing but invaluable encounter with ourselves.

111

The serpents and devils represent the dark side of the journey through the castle. They are the chief negative motif in *The Interior Castle*. They assault the pilgrimage from outside and they harass it from within. Even though a difficult hurdle is overcome when the individual begins the inner journey whole-heartedly, the outer pressures continue to be present in a detrimental way. And the inner journey reveals problems that were unknown prior to the beginning of the journey. At no stage of the journey is one totally free from possible attacks by the serpents and devils.

Serpents in the Castle

I am using "serpent" as a generic name for a host of creeping, crawling things that populate the outer environs, the walls, and many of the rooms of the castle. Teresa presents a cast of creatures representing a variety of concerns. But in general, the creatures are preoccupations which pull one away from God. Souls who are involved in external matters and do not practice prayer "are now so used to dealing always with the insects and vermin that are in the wall surrounding the castle that they have become almost like them."[1] One who is occupied with interior things has found "a good safeguard against falling and carrying on in this way like brute beasts."[2] Entering the castle is no safeguard either, because, initially, "so many reptiles get in with them that they are prevented from seeing the beauty of the castle and from calming down."[3]

In one passage in the first dwelling place Teresa marshals these images of darkness:

> You must note that hardly any of the light coming from the King's royal chamber reaches these first dwelling places. Even though they are not dark and black, as when the soul is in sin, they nevertheless are in some way darkened so that the soul cannot see the light. The darkness is not caused by a flaw in the room—for I don't know how to explain myself—but by

so many bad things like snakes and vipers and poisonous creatures that enter with the soul and don't allow it
to be aware of the light. It's as if a person were to enter
a place where the sun is shining but be hardly able to
open his eyes because of the mud in them. The room is
bright but he doesn't enjoy it because of the impedi-
ment of things like these wild animals or beasts that
make him close his eyes to everything but them. So, I
think, must be the condition of the soul. Even though it
may not be in a bad state, it is so involved in worldly
things and so absorbed with its possessions, honor, or
business affairs, as I have said, that even though as a
matter of fact it would want to see and enjoy its beauty
these things do not allow it to; nor does it seem that it
can slip free from so many impediments. If a person is
to enter the second dwelling place, it is important that
he strive to give up unnecessary things and business affairs.[4]

Difficulties with the serpents continue in the second dwelling place but the individual is making attempts to escape from
"snakes and poisonous creatures." Yet, success is not always possible because "these beasts are so poisonous and their presence
so dangerous and noisy that it would be a wonder if we kept
from stumbling and falling over them."[5]

Teresa prods people in the third dwelling place to hurry
along. She reasons that if a journey can be made quickly in a few
days, why take a year traveling through terrible weather on bad
roads. "Wouldn't it be better to make the journey all at once?"
she asks. "For all these obstacles are present, as well as danger
from snakes."[6]

Not even in the very last dwelling place can a person count
on an end to the dangers. Although it is rare, sometimes the
Lord allows such attacks so that the person will appreciate the
tremendous favors it usually receives. Teresa explains the experience of the attacks this way: "For sometimes our Lord leaves
these individuals in their natural state, and then it seems that all

the poisonous creatures from the outskirts and other dwelling places of this castle band together to take revenge for the time they were unable to have these souls under their control."[7]

The journey through the rooms and gardens of the beautiful castle begins to sound like a trip down the Amazon through insects, animals, vermin, reptiles, beasts, and snakes. Principally, these forces of darkness press in against the castle from the outside, and they are more numerous in the early stages of the trip. Teresa raises these images, which I am summing up as "serpents," to warn of the insidious and debilitating nature of outer fascinations which sap the inner journey. In this sense, the serpents represent the collective forces which have a hold on the individual. The outer adaptation in the first half of the individuation process resulted in an entry into a collective consciousness. Movement through the castle represents a move out of the collective into an individuating stance. The power of the collective over the individual is considerable. "Unconscious gregariousness is just animal," Jung said, "and with it goes the famous kind of thinking that causes people to worry night and day over what would be good for the eleven thousand virgins but never to bother about themselves. . . ."[8]

The extrovert, in particular, can more easily identify with a persona because the extrovert by nature is better attuned to the outer world. To disengage from these forces, the serpents, could be a difficult process. The introvert, too, may be caught up in the collective consciousness of the environment, but the introvert is not as comfortable with a persona as is the extrovert. Because the introvert tends to look within, her persona appears more artificial and awkward.[9] In either case, excessive commitment to collective ideals leads to a breakdown of the persona. In Teresa's imagery, the call of the King in the center of the castle barely pierces the noise of the serpents. He calls, she writes, "like a good shepherd, with a whistle so gentle that even they themselves almost fail to hear it. . . ."[10]

The castle becomes a fortress against the outside forces. It is a magic circle keeping chaos outside while a creation takes place inside. The mandala of the castle is a symbol of the self calling and orienting the human psyche as it walks the path of individuation. The dark forces outside press against the developing individual. The circle must not be broken. The problem becomes more complex, however, when the individual, finally closing the door on the serpents outside in the darkness, turns and sees them waiting in the inner rooms.

Serpents in the Psyche

The serpent image refers to more than the outer collective forces. The serpents are also met within the human psyche as the individual descends into the unconscious and contacts transpersonal layers of psyche. The collective unconscious is a powerful realm containing energies which can be overwhelming. The individuation process requires a delicate balance between opening oneself to the contents of the unconscious and at the same time maintaining a base in consciousness so that the contents may be integrated into conscious personality.

The reason for the descent into the unconscious in the first place is to bring the light of consciousness into that darkness. If the contents of these depths are not consciously met and allowed room in the personality, they may control the personality in an unconscious manner. Archetypes may be destructive if they are unconsciously lived out. One may be possessed by archetypes.

For example, one who unconsciously identifies with the God-archetype begins to exaggerate her worth and powers. The resulting behavior becomes destructive. Or when the archetypes are projected onto others or into the environment, as most contents of the unconscious are, we then unconsciously give our powers away and again become controlled by them. For example, Jung believed that the initial stages of falling in love involve being fascinated by archetypes which we unconsciously project on one another.

The coming of consciousness into these depths during the individuation process allows the archetypes to nourish the personality and energize it, without the person being overwhelmed or controlled by them. The serpent is an image which symbolizes these inner collective forces and speaks to the necessity of an ongoing struggle even within the castle itself.

Carl Jung's observations led him to conclude that images of animals which the psyche produced referred to the instinctual forces at work in the human personality. He said that "the dark animals like snakes, moles, mice, and the aquatic animals symbolize the heavy dark things. They can denote sexuality, and all sorts of earthly desires or instincts or emotions, because usually the emotions are supposed to be located in a sphere below the brain, either in the heart, or still lower in the abdomen. . . ."[11] He also said, "The serpent, as a soul, represents the lower strata of the human personality, the cold-blooded animal, the animal of the darkness, of the spinal cord and the solar plexus."[12] In the individuation process, communication is begun with this realm so that the individual may be connected to these depths and own the wider, integrated life that is possible. Without this communication, these depths may disrupt the personality, or, in symbolic language, the serpents may bite and poison the individual.[13]

The human personality begins in the unconscious, and this state has been symbolized as a snake biting its own tail, a circular serpent. This serpent is an ambiguous figure because it does symbolize the unconscious beginnings of the emerging personality, but it also represents the power of the unconscious to drag down fragile consciousness and swallow it in its depths. The image of St. George fighting the dragon is a symbolic portrayal of ego-consciousness fighting to be free of the unconscious, not only as the ego first emerges from the unconscious, but also later when a descent into the unconscious is part of the journey to the self. But the serpent is ambiguous, and the dangers must be faced if the positive, healing power of the serpent is also to be experienced.

So, while Teresa cannot stand the serpents in the castle, there is a positive side to their presence which she intuitively acknowledges. This positive side was discussed by Jung as he commented on the following fantasy sent to him by a woman: "I beheld a Gothic cathedral with high spires. A great religious procession was entering the church chanting a Te Deum. A small grotesque animal like a gargoyle kept clutching at the gold robe of the priest. The priest tried to kick it away but could not. I entered the cathedral with the procession. The priest ascended the steps to the altar and lifted on high the sacred chalice. As he did so small animals and frogs leapt forth from it."[14]

Jung interpreted the psyche as saying that the way to wholeness involves the chthonic, earthy elements of life. The way up is the way down. The Gothic cathedral is an image in architecture of an upward striving. The priest, the gold robes, and the chalice all speak of higher things. And yet, present among all the splendor are the lower things, the frogs and their friends.

Cathedrals actually do incorporate the images of gargoyles and other grotesque animals. They are found not only on the outside walls but even on the choir stalls within the sanctuary. Gnomes and dwarfs, frogs and lizards, and those things that live in the roots of trees, or in caves, or under bridges, have a place in the magnificent edifices of medieval Christianity. The grotesque character is a type of wisdom figure which mocks our efforts to deny our rootedness in the earth. The psyche that leaves the earth to float in space is reminded of its need to keep in touch with the ground.

One example of the helpful nature of instincts was related by Jung in a story about a woman who had moods of depression. She was quite dependent upon Jung—too much so, he felt. He decided to go on vacation, and she warned that if he did leave, her moods might prove too much for her to bear. Jung left anyway, and true to her warning, she began a march down to the lake to jump in. On her way to the lake she passed a shoe store. When she glanced in the window, a particular pair of shoes caught her eye. She stopped, went into the store, tried on the shoes, and in a few minutes emerged from the store wearing the new pair of shoes. Her depression was completely gone, so she went back home. Jung commented: "If I had put a mountain under her feet it would not have cured her but that pair of shoes could do it."[15] He advised her to buy another pair when the next mood came upon her, and he reports that on the next occasion she did buy something equally foolish.

The story involves a serious problem, but has an almost whimsical solution. Jung likened her situation to stories of the hero who finds himself in a predicament. Suddenly, one or two little animals appear and lead the hero to safety. His point is that things very near and evident are often overlooked, things such as the instincts. Buying the shoes was an instinctual action. The woman made no conscious connection between the shoes and her depression. Her normal conscious understandings and convictions had deserted her, and so she did a childish thing. And that grounding in her nature started a healing process.

The image of the frog, in particular, spoke to Jung of the ambiguity of human development. The frog is cold-blooded and lives partly on land, but is also still immersed in the primeval waters. It represents the biological aspect of the human condition. It also represents the promise of the possibility of growing into a warm-blooded, fully human, interiorized person. We humans are partly immersed in the primeval waters of the unconscious and we cannot forget this condition without hurting ourselves. In those waters is where it all begins.

The frogs that jumped from the chalice in the Gothic cathedral were a healing symbol. They were an invitation to the individual to accept herself as she is. "Wisdom begins," Jung said, "when we take things as they are; otherwise we get nowhere."[16] The following comments, also, are well-worded:

Man is in an exceedingly embryonic state, and the superior man can never develop when the tadpoles decide they are not tadpoles but something much more wonderful, when they deny that they have tails and fins, when the frogs pretend that they have warm blood and beautiful singing voices. First we must accept the fact of ourselves, what we are; then we can develop. In accepting ourselves in our embryonic condition we receive ourselves, as a mother receives a child in her womb where it is fed and develops. If we can really accept ourselves, we can feed and develop ourselves; to expect anything else is like expecting a cast-off child to thrive.[17]

Teresa's presentation of the serpents in the castle is psychologically subtle. True, she emphasizes the negative aspect of the serpents, especially as they represent outer attractions which war against the inner journey she is advocating. On the other hand, she hints that meeting and struggling with the serpents in the castle is not without its redeeming features. This attitude is clearly seen as she talks about the other forces of evil in the castle, the devils. Teresa's instinctive acceptance of the dark side of the journey is, perhaps, a tribute to her own self-acceptance.

The Devils and Jung's Shadow Concept

Behind the serpents in the castle stand the devils, a personification of the threats to a successful journey. It is really the devils who are waging the war in the castle, and they do not concede a single room of the "million" or so rooms in the first dwelling place. Teresa warns that the devil is so determined that "he must have in each room many legions of devils to fight souls off when they try to go from one room to the other."[18] And the devils are even more active in the second dwelling place. The war is fierce and the devils use the serpents as their troops. "The blows from the artillery strike in such a way that the soul cannot fail to hear. It is in this stage that the devils represent these snakes (worldly things) and the temporal pleasures of the present as though almost eternal."[19] Teresa calls for a "manly" fight against the devils in order to conquer them. They are everywhere, and not even souls in union with God may relax against the devil. "There is no enclosure so fenced in that he cannot enter, or desert so withdrawn that he fails to go there."[20]

The devil is the traditional figure used to indicate the source of evil. He is the tempter who leads us into destructiveness. Psychologically, this figure is one of the many used by the psyche in its personification of the neglected, negative aspects of personality. Jung called this dark figure in the human psyche the *shadow*. He wrote: "Unfortunately there can be no doubt that man is, on the whole, less good than he imagines himself or wants to be. Everyone carries a shadow, and the less it is embodied in the individual's conscious life, the blacker and denser it is."[21] The shadow side of the personality is one of Jung's more intriguing theories. It provides a framework for discussing the possible sources of destruction in the psyche. And, surprisingly, it points to avenues of growth.

In general, the shadow dwells in the personal unconscious and represents that aspect of personality which an individual is ashamed of, or will not recognize because it is unacceptable to the conscious personality. It clashes with the conscious identity of a person. The shadow represents the past, the primitive and inferior parts of the self which have not been given the chance to dwell in the light. Desire and emotions are found in the shadow, and since the unconscious has a kind of autonomy, these emotions can have a possessive quality. The shadow is in touch with the serpent, collective layers of the psyche.

To handle the shadow requires sensitive care. It cannot be continually repressed since, in Jung's theory, psychic energy is only dammed up, never eliminated. And pent-up energy becomes destructive if channels are not available for expression. On the other hand, the presence of the shadow, particularly the more destructive aspects represented by that figure, does not mean that it must be lived out without regard for norms of morality. The shadow may be transformed into a positive source of energy for the personality, but first it must be admitted and accepted as a reality in the psyche.

The shadow contains not only negative elements and destructive possibilities, but also potential for greater growth and development of the personality. Jung found that the shadow is ninety percent gold. Although it is undeveloped and acts negatively, it is capable of being brought to light for the enrichment of personality. Much of what is in the shadow is the unlived life of the individual. This "positive" aspect of the shadow represents potential which could be tapped, but pressures, fears, or perhaps an unwillingness to take responsibility makes it difficult to "own" this part of the self.

The shadow contains the excess baggage not used by the ego in its development in the first phase of the individuation process. As a person develops ego-consciousness and adopts a persona, one of the attitude-types predominates and the other takes up residence in the unconscious, lending a particular shape to the shadow. And as one of the four psychological functions becomes the predominant function, the other three find themselves in the unconscious in varying degrees. The function opposite the predominant function, called the inferior function, resides deepest in the unconscious and provides content for the shadow. It is apparent that as a person gets older, she casts a longer shadow.

An important way in which the shadow is recognized is in projection. Those things which we cannot abide in ourselves we project upon others. If I do not admit my shadow side I will unconsciously find another who will carry my shadow for me. Once this projection is made then I need not be upset with myself. My problems are now outside and I can fight them out there rather than within the real arena, myself. Projections give us an excuse for our bad behavior toward others. We can be aggressive, violent, and make war because the evil is clearly in the other, not ourselves. It is no easy task to bring our troops home and to learn to own our own shadow. Jung commented on this difficulty: "While some traits peculiar to the shadow can be recognized without too much difficulty as one's own personal qualities, in this case both insight and good will are unavailing because the cause of the emotion appears to lie, beyond all possibility of doubt, in the *other person*. No matter how obvious it may be to the neutral observer that it is a matter of projections, there is little hope that the subject will perceive this himself. He must be convinced that he throws a very long shadow before he is willing to withdraw his emotionally-toned projections from their object."[22]

It is the very presence of this emotion which offers a clue to projected material. In general, extreme or inappropriate emotion accompanies an unconscious projection. Rage, fear, even admiration can be signs that projection is taking place. In those instances we are giving away parts of our self. The person who has unowned strengths, and always greatly admires them in another, is doing herself a disservice. She is letting others carry the gifts, accomplish the goals, which she herself has the power to do. Thus the emotion accompanying a projection may be positive or negative. And it is the emotion which makes integrating the shadow into consciousness a difficult task.

The shadow must be experienced to be truly accepted. When the shadow is merely intellectually acknowledged, it is still being kept away. To feel the repulsiveness of the negative contents of the shadow and to admit that they belong to oneself is a disturbing process. Jolande Jacobi writes:

> It is in ourselves that we most frequently and readily perceive shadow qualities, provided we are willing to acknowledge them as belonging to ourselves; for example, when an outburst of rage comes over us, when suddenly we begin to curse or behave crudely, when quite against our will we act antisocially, when we are stingy, petty, or choleric, cowardly, frivolous, or hypocritical, so displaying qualities which under ordinary circumstances we carefully hide or repress and of whose existence we ourselves are unaware. When the emergence of such traits of character can no longer be overlooked, we ask ourselves in amazement: How was it possible? Is it really true that things like this are me?[23]

The challenge is to be a good samaritan to myself. But it is difficult to "befriend" that which may be repugnant.

The descent into the unconscious soon involves an encounter with the shadow since this figure is generally the first of the inner figures which will be met. One form of the shadow is personal and consists of psychic features which are practically the opposite of the conscious persona. This shadow would be met immediately in the personal unconscious. In dreams, a figure of the same sex as the dreamer will generally represent the shadow.

Another form of the shadow is more archetypal and collective. It does not relate so much to the individual as it does to the dark side of humankind in general. It is often the underside of the prevailing times, the neglected side of the culture. Myths and fairy tales present figures from this level of the unconscious.

Horror stories, too, express the collective shadow. Some of the figures, such as sharks, ants, and birds, exemplify the impersonal, primitive nature of this shadow.

The collective shadow is particularly harmful when it is projected upon a minority in a land. The majority then meets its unacceptable dark side in the minority and reacts to the minority with the fear and hatred which the shadow engenders. The extreme, and often violent, reaction to the minority surprises everyone by its intensity. Perhaps this potential for destructiveness found deep in the human psyche is what Jung referred to as "absolute evil" when he wrote: "With a little self-criticism one can see through the shadow—so far as its nature is personal. But when it appears as an archetype, one encounters the same difficulties as with anima and animus. In other words, it is quite within the bounds of possibility for man to recognize the relative evil of his nature, but it is a rare and shattering experience for him to gaze into the face of absolute evil."[24]

Teresa's analysis of the castle journey demonstrates an awareness of the shadow and impersonal regions of the personality. The devils and serpents will be encountered, and that is a fact of life in the castle. They are unwanted and uninvited, and yet in an ironic way the castle is their home too.

Entering the Shadows of the Castle

Teresa warned her sisters about concentrating on the faults of one another and missing their own darkness. Not only does the individual sister remain ignorant of her own weaknesses, but the charity which should characterize relationships in the convent will cool. "What the devil is hereby aiming after is no small thing: the cooling of the charity and love the Sisters have for one another. This would cause serious harm. Let us understand, my daughters, that true perfection consists in love of God and neighbor; the more perfectly we keep these two commandments, the more perfect we will be. All that is in our rule and constitutions serves for nothing else than to be a means toward keeping these commandments with greater perfection." And then Teresa shows great insight into the shadow: "Let's forget about indiscreet zeal; it can do us a lot of harm. Let each one look to herself."[25] Teresa admits that others may have faults and corrections may have to be made, but the primary responsibility for the individual is to attend to this inner journey which will reveal one's own neglected areas. In the terms of psychology, Teresa is warning against projecting one's shadow upon others. With so much zeal in the convent, so much striving for ideals, an equal amount of negative material may be constellated in the unconscious. And "indiscreet zeal" will refuse to acknowledge this shadow side. Consequently, others will become scapegoats.

Again, Teresa, in her own way, is sensitive to what can be learned when the shadow is projected: "Let us look at our own faults and leave aside those of others, for it is very characteristic of persons with such well-ordered lives to be shocked by everything. Perhaps we could truly learn from the one who shocks us what is most important even though we may surpass him in external composure and our way of dealing with others."[26] Teresa's caution to those who live well-ordered lives brings to mind Jung's comment on the dangers of high noon. When the sun is directly overhead, no shadow is cast. When a person lives totally in the light of consciousness and its smug perception, the dark side finds no place for expression and acts out of control. Others catch the shadow projection, and so become sources of learning about the self.

Teresa's call for insight into oneself rather than criticism of others is a call to bring the war home and endure the conflict in one's own backyard as it were. The war is difficult but, in its own way, necessary and even helpful. She writes: "I hold that the situation is much better in this stage of prayer when these creatures do enter and wage war, for the devil could deceive one with respect to the spiritual delights given by God if there were no temptations, and do much more harm than when temptations are felt."[27] Teresa recognizes that it is better to face reality, to experience and *feel* the dark forces which are present. These struggles are healthy in the long run: "For when a soul is in one continual state, I don't consider it safe, nor do I think it is possible for the spirit of the Lord to be in one fixed state during this exile."[28]

Teresa has deeply experienced the fact that the inner journey brings struggles unique to itself. Closing the door of the castle on the outer preoccupations and setting off for the center is a
step into the reality of a fragmented inner world. Teresa observes: "It seems to me that all the contempt and trials one can
endure in life cannot be compared to these interior battles. Any
disquiet and war can be suffered if we find peace where we live,
as I have already said. But that we desire to rest from the thousand trials there are in the world and that the Lord wants to prepare us for tranquillity and that within ourselves lies the
obstacle to such rest and tranquillity cannot fail to be very painful and almost unbearable."[29] Teresa continually emphasizes
the strangeness of the interior life. It is fundamentally an unknown world and the experience of this terrain is a disconcerting encounter for the person who thinks she knows herself.
Teresa stresses that being out of touch with oneself brings about
the experience of conflict:

> O Lord, take into account the many things we suffer on
> this path for lack of knowledge! The trouble is that
> since we do not think there is anything to know other
> than that we must think of You, we do not even know
> how to ask those who know nor do we understand
> what there is to ask. Terrible trials are suffered because
> we don't understand ourselves, and that which isn't
> bad at all but good we think is a serious fault. This lack
> of knowledge causes the afflictions of many people who
> engage in prayer: complaints about interior trials, at
> least to a great extent, by people who have no learning;
> melancholy and loss of health; and even the complete
> abandonment of prayer. For such persons don't reflect
> that there is an interior world here within us. . . . For
> the most part all the trials and disturbances come from
> our not understanding ourselves.[30]

Carl Jung's psychology suggests that a chief source of conflict during the individuation process is the encounter with the
neglected areas of personality, the shadow. These underdevel-

oped, inferior, troublesome areas shock ego-consciousness and place hurdles in the path to the self. When Teresa encourages an inner journey and the initial experiences are distasteful, what motivation is there to go on? What attraction can there be to coming home to oneself when that home is not felt to be a good and comfortable place? The resolution of the shadow problem is a difficult and necessary step which is a premise for the rest of the journey. I cannot move toward the self while I am loathing the self I am experiencing. Teresa gives an indication of this suspicion of the self: "These miseries will not afflict or assail everyone as much as they did me for many years because of my wretchedness. It seems that I myself wanted to take vengeance on myself. And since it was something so painful for me, I think perhaps that it will be so for you too."[31]

Teresa is speaking specifically about thoughts which distract from prayer and the general state of unrecollectedness that is found within the person. Jung's shadow theory suggests that she is also speaking of the experience of the psychic debris of the shadow and the confusion which results when rejected parts of the personality are encountered. Teresa maintains that we have to come to know ourselves and that ignorance of the self is the real source of conflict. From a depth psychology viewpoint Jung reinforces Teresa. Without entrance into the unconscious, the shadow eventually disrupts the personality and the environment in which the person lives. Without a conscious entrance into the collective layers of the psyche and a return with greater consciousness and awareness, the individual receives no nourishment for growth, and the self remains only a dream. And without conscious appropriation and integration, the archetypal forces deep in the psyche become the enemy of wholeness with their numinosity. They will attract and possess with a blind force and the personality will begin to detour in its development.

While Teresa certainly does not use these psychological terms, her images of serpents and devils lead to such conclusions. There is always a danger of twisting her words to fit a theory, but there is also a danger of limiting her experiences to her words. An exploration and amplification of the serpent and devil images allows us to enter into her experiences more fully. The premise is that the human psyche generally uses such images to symbolize certain depth experiences. Jung has identified these experiences as the entrance into the collective, archetypal layers of the unconscious, and the encounter with the shadow side of personality.

A Princess, A Castle, A Frog

Fairytales provided Jung with a wealth of images for his study of the psyche. These timeless stories are often expressive of fundamental psychic issues and provide a window to the soul.[32] An archetypal drama lurks in Teresa's encounter with the serpents in the castle. The following fairytale, recounted by the Brothers Grimm, appears to be rooted in the same archetypal, transpersonal level of human experience. The story helps fix Teresa's journey in the wider human journey. It is titled "The Frog-King, or Iron Henry":

> In olden times when wishing still helped one, there lived a king whose daughters were all beautiful, but the youngest was so beautiful that the sun itself, which has seen so much, was astonished whenever it shone in her face. Close by the old lime-tree in the forest was a well, and when the day was very warm, the King's child went out into the forest and sat down by the side of the cool fountain; and when she was bored she took a golden ball, and threw it up on high and caught it; and this ball was her favorite plaything.

On one occasion, however, she did not catch the ball. It fell to the ground and rolled into the well. She tried looking into the well to see the golden ball but the waters were too deep and the ball had vanished. The princess began to cry, and she cried louder and louder. Suddenly a voice interrupted her grief: "What ails you, King's daughter? You weep so that even a stone would show pity." She turned and saw a frog sticking its head out of the water. "Ah! old water-splasher, is it you? I am weeping for my golden ball, which has fallen into the well."

The frog said that he could help her, but he wanted to know what she would give him in return. She promised to give him anything, even the crown on her head. The frog said that what he really wanted was to be her companion. He wanted to sit at table with her, eat off her plate, drink from her cup, and then sleep in her bed. If she promised to give him these things, he would go below the waters and bring up the golden ball.

The princess promised. But in her mind she was thinking that no frog could be a proper companion for a human being; the frog was being silly. The frog went down into the waters of the well and soon appeared with the golden ball in his mouth. He threw it on the grass. The King's daughter picked up the ball and ran away. "Wait, wait," said the frog. "Take me with you. I can't run as you can." But the princess ran home, and soon forgot about the frog in the well.

The following evening, while the princess, the King, and all his courtiers were having supper, the frog splish-splashed to the castle and knocked on the door. The princess opened the door, saw the frog and became frightened, and slammed the door. She went back to the table. But the King asked her about the incident, and she told him about her promises to the frog. The King told her that she had to be true to her promises, so she let the frog in the door. The frog followed her to the table, sat on the table, and began eating from her plate. The princess lost her appetite.

When the meal was finished, the frog said, "I have eaten and am satisfied; now I am tired; carry me into your little room and make your little silken bed ready, and we will both lie down and go to sleep." The King's daughter began to cry, but the King reminded her that the frog had helped her and should not be despised now. Therefore she took the frog to her room but put him in one corner of the room while she went to bed. The frog crept up to her and said: "I am tired. I want to sleep as well as you. Lift me up or I will tell your father." The princess became very angry. She picked up the frog and hurled it against the wall. "Now will you be quiet, odious frog!" she said. But when the frog fell to the floor it was no longer a frog but "a king's son with kind and beautiful eyes."

The prince told her that he had been bewitched by a wicked witch and put in the well. Only the princess could have saved him. The two became husband and wife and the prince promised that in the morning he would take her to his kingdom. The next day a carriage arrived driven by faithful Henry, the servant of the prince. Henry had been so unhappy when his master was bewitched that he had three iron bands placed around his heart so that it would not burst with grief.

As the couple were driving off in the carriage they heard a cracking sound. The prince cried: "Henry, the carriage is breaking."

> "No, master, it is not the carriage. It is a band from my heart, which was put there in my great pain when you were a frog and imprisoned in the well." Again and once again while they were on their way something cracked, and each time the King's son thought the carriage was breaking; but it was only the bands which were springing from the heart of faithful Henry because his master was set free and was happy.[33]

Concluding Reflections and Suggestions

The images of the serpents and devils introduce the reader of *The Interior Castle* to the battles within the castle. While the serpents and devils are to be defeated, Teresa admits that it is good to feel the heat of the battle rather than to presumptuously think that all is well with oneself. The intensity of the struggle, she believes, is due to the fact that we do not really know ourselves. The journey through the castle is a journey into our own reality.

Carl Jung's depth psychology supports Teresa's belief that a struggle is necessary. Jung wrote, "There is no birth of consciousness without pain."[34] The inner world is unlike the outer in many respects, but both are objective worlds which may smother the fragile life of one who is attempting to be an individual, to follow the law of her own being. The serpents are a reminder that the inner journey must be made with care. The descent is to be made with the light of consciousness so that treasures may be illumined and retrieved. Otherwise, the darkness is confusing and engulfing. The unconscious life of an individual is the womb where rebirth may take place, but it is also the place where a person may be bewitched, caught in collective, instinctual living.

Recently I met an impressive group of people who worked with individuals who were losing their battle with inner demons. This group was part of a staff which operates residential treatment centers for severely schizophrenic adolescents. One of them described schizophrenia to me as a situation of split or fragmented heart and mind. The inner demons, the unconscious forces, seriously disturbed or were in control of the personality. This staff daily witnessed the destructive power, the hold which the collective forces of the psyche had on the young people.

But along with the reality of the destructive aspects of the psyche, the staff also witnessed the ability of the human psyche to heal itself and to continue to develop along healthy channels. Through the use of images, stories, and ritual, the staff provided archetypal environments which spoke to the collective unconscious levels of the broken psyches. In particular the staff used American Indian stories, and rituals involving nature and the change of seasons. In the mornings the staff facilitated dream sessions where the images of the night could be shared.

In these and other ways the fragmented personalities of the adolescents were exposed to images and stories which might help them continue with their own stalled story. The staff provided archetypal symbols which helped the young people face their demons and emerge into the light of consciousness. The staff named their treatment centers after St. George because their work was a battle with the dragons of the unconscious.

This journey of descent into the unconscious is difficult to avoid, in Jung's estimation. We have a choice of descending carefully, carrying a torch and watching our step, or we will back off the cliff unknowingly. The inevitability of inner conflict was emphasized by Jung when he said that the right way as well as the wrong way must be paid for. Teresa's pilgrim in the third dwelling place is caught in just such a dilemma. To stay put is to experience an unraveling of a carefully constructed life; but to move on forces an encounter with inner demons.

Conscious and careful attention to the individuation process is not always a necessary condition for the emergence of the self. People certainly grow into their wider lives without knowing the terminology and the dynamics of the individuation process. A deep faith and an attentiveness to God in her life brought Teresa to the center of her castle. Her service of others expressed and helped shape her life's direction.

For other people, the journey is just never begun. Jung wrote: "To the extent that a man is untrue to the law of his being and does not rise to personality, he has failed to realize his life's meaning. Fortunately in her kindness and patience, Nature never puts the fatal question as to the meaning of their lives into the mouths of most people. And where no one asks, no one need answer."[35]

But in many lives, and especially today, the individuation process is calling attention to itself. Developmental studies are providing a topography of the human journey. And attention is being called to predictable struggles. For example, one study attempts to name some of the polarities which are experienced in the mid-life transition: young/old, creative/destructive, outer/inner, and masculine/feminine.[36] Relationships between men and women, and within families, give evidence of psychic strain. The powerfully destructive potential within the depths of the psyche has been witnessed in fanatical mass movements where leaders and followers unconsciously live out archetypal dramas. As has been pointed out, psychology did not bring about these conditions; today's conditions emphasize the need for a continuing and deepening study of the human psyche. In Jung's words, we are "pitifully ignorant" of the psyche.

The shadow concept provides a helpful handle on an important dimension of the individuation process. Initially the inner journey is exciting and stimulating. But the adventure soon loses its attractiveness when the shadow side and its unwanted figures, such as the devils, appear. "At these moments," writes James Hillman, a Jungian analyst, "when one meets face to face the perverse and amoral creatures who have been inhabiting other parts of the building, the homilies which are usually understood by us in terms of how to be with others become lessons of how to be with ourselves."[37]

Often there is not as much support for loving ourselves as there is for loving others. The shadow is the humiliating and socially unacceptable part of myself. And yet movement to the self requires that I invite all of these inner figures to the banquet of my life, because they are already a part of that life. Love of self necessitates caring for the shadow. It cannot be driven away by exhortation or moralizing. I do not have to identify with the shadow or act it out, but loving the shadow will mean befriending and carrying it. The acceptance of our reality is true humility. "For never," writes Teresa, "however exalted the soul may be, is anything else more fitting than self-knowledge; nor could it be even were the soul to so desire. For humility, like the bee making honey in the beehive, is always at work. Without it, everything goes wrong."[38] Caring for the shadow is the prerequisite for curing it.

When I teach Jung's shadow concept in class I often show the old, silent film version of Victor Hugo's novel, *The Hunchback of Notre Dame*. The hunchback is the bell-ringer in the Cathedral of Notre Dame in Paris during the reign of Louis XI. He scrambles in the towers of the cathedral and taunts the people below who give him little thought and no respect. He is a neglected, outcast figure who, at the same time, serves the sacred place and loves the music of the bells.

The hunchback is wrongly accused of a crime and is publicly punished, to the delight of the crowd. The rejected, hated figure being whipped and insulted is a moving image.

A young woman in the crowd reacts differently from the others. Rather than being frightened or repulsed by the bell-ringer, she shows a sensitive compassion. She alone remains with the pathetic figure and comforts him after his punishment. This caring gesture touches the hunchback deeply even as it amazes him. He had never received this type of treatment.

Later, when the woman is in danger at the hands of the villain of the story, the hunchback gives his own life to save her. Also, he had just helped defend the cathedral from an attacking mob.

As old as the film is, the hunchback leaves an indelible image in the viewer's mind. Within the despised, alienated figure of the bell-ringer is a nobility which guards the sacred and saves the life of another person.

I used to play a tape during the silent film. The tape explained the theory of the shadow concept. But no one listened. The images and story were too engrossing. Besides, the message was clear: accepting and loving the rejected shadow in our depths is the beginning of healing and wholeness for the personality.

The positive aspect of the shadow is as demanding as the negative aspect. It is far easier to remain ignorant of one's giftedness and let others take responsibility. The individuation process is a journey of awareness, and with awareness comes responsibility. The positive shadow challenges me to own and live out of parts of the personality which will often separate me from the collective. Jung emphasized the comfortableness of collective living, and the heroism involved in allowing oneself to be led out of that collective. Reality includes not only our destructive capabilities, but also the contributions that are ours to make to the wider life around us. That, too, is humility.

A Christian community, if it is honestly Christian, will be comfortable with the shadow. Such a community does not offer the absence of shadow as a sign of its Christianity, but its willingness to carry the shadow in acceptance and forgiveness. Many of Jesus' meals were with the shadow figures of his times. The Christian community, too, will enable the recognition and ownership of the gifts of the members. As a contemporary theologian writes, "Christian commitment is a question of fused purpose of many people gifted for mission out of their shared experience."[39] As the community facilitates life passages, such as the encounter with the shadow, through its symbols, the individuals renew and deepen their commitment to the community and its mission. Teresa's criterion for the authenticity of the castle journey is the quality of mission which results from the growing conformity with God's will.

The serpents and devils represent experiences of disorientation for the soul entering the inner world. But the skins of these repellent creatures may cover something quite appealing and healing, as with the frog-prince. A striking Teresian image of healing and new life is the butterfly. The butterfly's story is the story of the psyche and the birth of the self through successive passages. It is the next image to be explored.

NOTES

1. *Interior Castle*, I, chap. 1, no. 6.
2. Ibid., I, chap. 1, no. 7.
3. Ibid., I, chap. 1, no. 8.
4. Ibid., I, chap. 2, no. 14.
5. Ibid., II, chap. 1, no. 2.
6. Ibid., III, chap. 2, no. 7.
7. Ibid., VII, chap. 4, no. 1.
8. Jung, *Visions*, vol. 1, p. 89.
9. Jolande Jacobi, *Masks of the Soul* (Grand Rapids: William B. Eerdmans Publishing Co., 1976), p. 54.
10. *Interior Castle*, IV, chap. 3, no. 2.
11. Jung, *Visions*, vol. 1, p. 31.
12. Ibid., p. 198.
13. Cf. Jung, C.W., XVI, 472.
14. Jung, *Visions*, vol. 1, p. 195.
15. Ibid., p. 54.
16. Ibid., p. 203.
17. Ibid., pp. 203, 4.
18. *Interior Castle*, I, chap. 2, no. 12.
19. Ibid., II, chap. 1, no. 3.
20. Ibid., V, chap. 4, no. 8.
21. Jung, Ibid., XI, 131.
22. Ibid., IXii, 16.
23. Jacobi, *The Psychology of C.G. Jung*, p. 111.
24. Jung, C.W., IXii, 19.
25. *Interior Castle*, I, chap. 2, no. 17.
26. Ibid., III, chap. 2, no. 13.

27. Ibid., IV, chap. 1, no. 3.

28. Ibid.

29. Ibid., IV, chap. 1, no. 12.

30. Ibid., IV, chap. 1, no. 9.

31. Ibid., IV, chap. 1, no. 13.

32. Marie Louise von Franz, a colleague of Jung's and an analyst, has extensively studied fairytales. She writes: "Fairy tales are the purest and simplest expression of collective unconscious psychic processes. Therefore their value for the scientific investigation of the unconscious exceeds that of all other material. They represent the archetypes in their simplest, barest and most concise form. In this pure form, the archetypal images afford us the best clues to the understanding of the processes going on in the collective psyche. In myths or legends, or any other more elaborate mythological material, we get at the basic patterns of the human psyche through an overlay of cultural material. But in fairy tales there is much less specific conscious cultural material and therefore they mirror the basic patterns of the psyche more clearly": *Interpretation of Fairytales* (Zurich: Spring Publications, 1970), p. 1.

33. *The Complete Grimm's Fairytales* (New York: Pantheon Books, 1972), pp. 17–20.

34. Jung, C.W., XVII, 331.

35. Ibid., 314.

36. Daniel Levinson, *Seasons of a Man's Life* (New York: Alfred A. Knopf, 1978), pp. 197ff.

37. James Hillman, *Insearch: Psychology and Religion* (New York: Charles Scribner's Sons, 1967), p. 73.

38. *Interior Castle*, I, chap. 2, no. 8.

39. Regis Duffy, "Unreasonable Expectations" in *Proceedings of the Catholic Theological Society of America*, vol. 34, 1979. Duffy discusses the relationship of life-passages to Church, sacraments, and commitment. In a summary of one part he writes: "I simply submit that worthwhile conflict and consequent commitment is more than a question of psychological congruence for theology. God's continuing salvific action in us is the radical cause of the conflicts which question our deepest motivations and meanings. Sacrament is one symbolized expression of such action and our communal and individual response. Commitment to evangelical mission tests the effectiveness of such symbols for us" (pp. 16–17).

CHAPTER SIX

Butterfly, An Image of Healing

The psyche has a remarkable ability to weather the storms of life and to renew itself. In all of our deep transitions, our crises and conversions, we are challenged to let go of something so that something else may be born. These occasions are periods of great confusion and hurt. Often we feel alone in our collapsing world.

Somewhere, deep down, a healing process begins which slowly mends the shattered psyche and gives strength for renewed living. The source of healing is a mystery. But we know that a door has opened where we thought only a wall existed.

The image of the butterfly represents for many people the fresh and beautiful, but fragile, life which appears just when the cocoon of darkness appears to be a permanent state. The butterfly signifies the healing power found in our depths.

Teresa of Avila used the butterfly to symbolize the healing which is experienced in union with God. Jung saw in the image of the butterfly the healing power of the psyche as the self emerges through transformations.

Jung wrote that the butterfly is a theriomorphic symbol of the self.[1] Its story is an allegory for the story of the psyche.[2] For the self to emerge, ego-consciousness must enter the darkness of the unconscious. The prior conscious attitude gives way in a relationship to the depths, and a new consciousness develops. The psyche finds the metamorphosis of the butterfly an apt figuring of its own transformations.

In both the story of the butterfly and the heroes of mythology, the psyche recognizes its journey. Both silkworm and hero enter a region of danger. The descent is necessary because only in this realm will the treasure be found. The cocoon stage of the silkworm is the "night sea journey" of the hero. Just as the sun dies into the west and travels to the east in order to be born again, so the hero, so the worm, so the light of consciousness must make a descent into dark regions.

In *The Interior Castle* the appealing image of the butterfly is used by Teresa to picture the effects of union with God. The fifth dwelling place represents this beginning union which then intensifies and deepens in the experiences of the last two dwelling places. The image of the silkworm-cocoon-butterfly likewise is first used in the fifth dwelling place with the butterfly reappearing in the sixth and seventh dwelling places. The butterfly theme perdures through this second half of the castle journey along with the theme of marriage. The butterfly eventually "dies" in the last dwelling place as the image of Christ strongly emerges. Teresa introduces the image as she attempts to describe the effects of the prayer of union:

> To explain things better I want to use a helpful comparison; it is good for making us see how, even though we can do nothing in this work done by the Lord, we can do much by disposing ourselves so that His Majesty may grant us this favor.
>
> You must have already heard about His marvels manifested in the way silk originates, for only He could have invented something like that. The silkworms come from seeds about the size of little grains of pepper. (I have never seen this but have heard of it, and so if something in the explanation gets distorted it won't be my fault.) When the warm weather comes and the leaves begin to appear on the mulberry tree, the seeds start to live, for they are dead until then. The worms nourish themselves on the mulberry leaves un-

til, having grown to full size, they settle on some twigs. There with their little mouths they themselves go about spinning the silk and making some very thick little cocoons in which they enclose themselves. The silkworm, which is fat and ugly, then dies, and a little white butterfly, which is very pretty, comes forth from the cocoon.[3]

Teresa admits that she learned about this process through hearsay. She does not vouch for its accuracy in all the details. Her example is inaccurate in that it apparently confused moths and butterflies. Nevertheless, in each case there is a chrysalis, if not a cocoon, and the butterfly does emerge from the darkness of the chrysalis. In any event, we will use Teresa's images for the process, namely, silkworm-cocoon-butterfly.

This process is an image of the entire castle adventure. It has two stages linked by a transition as does the journey to the center of the castle. The growth of the silkworm corresponds to the beginning dwelling places. The nourishment of the mulberry leaves strengthens the silkworm just as meditation, reading good books, and hearing sermons help the soul to mature.

The inner movement toward God begins in earnest as the fully grown silkworm begins to contruct a cocoon. The cocoon hides the dark, interior processes of transformation, corresponding to the second stage of the castle journey. Building that cocoon requires intense effort:

Therefore, courage, my daughters! Let's be quick to do this work and weave this little cocoon by taking away our self-love and self-will, our attachment to any earthly thing, and by performing deeds of penance, prayer, mortification, obedience, and of all the other things you know. Would to heaven that we would do what we know we must; and we are instructed about what we must do. Let it die; let this silkworm die, as it does in completing what it was created to do! And you will see how we see God, as well as ourselves placed inside His grandeur, as is this little silkworm within its cocoon.[4]

Freeing oneself for a relationship with God produces a container for transformation. The relationship is the container, the cocoon, which allows for deep contact between the soul and God. The union with God in the inner depths is experienced as a liberation, and the butterfly-soul emerges.

> Now, then, let's see what this silkworm does, for that's the reason I've said everything else. When the soul is, in this prayer, truly dead to the world, a little white butterfly comes forth. O greatness of God! How transformed the soul is when it comes out of this prayer after having been placed within the greatness of God and so closely joined with Him for a little while—in my opinion the union never lasts for as much as a half hour. Truly, I tell you that the soul doesn't recognize itself. Look at the difference there is between an ugly worm and a little white butterfly; that's what the difference is here.[5]

This union with God produces strong effects which, Teresa guesses, do not last a half hour. She writes that "during the time that the union lasts the soul is left as though without its senses, for it has no power to think even if it wants to."[6] And she states that no techniques will produce this experience. Only after the experience can a judgment be made regarding its genuineness. "For during the time of this union it neither sees, nor hears, nor understands, because the union is always short and seems to the soul even much shorter than it probably is. God so places Himself in the interior of that soul that when it returns to itself it can in no way doubt that it was in God and God was in it."[7]

True union with God does not necessarily result in the phenomena or experiences Teresa is describing. She begins her description of the fifth dwelling place by saying that most people seriously engaged in prayer enter this dwelling place. But not all will experience what Teresa experienced. "There are various degrees," she writes, "and for that reason I say that most enter these places. But I believe that only a few will experience some of the things that I will say are in this room."[8] Beneath the various experiences in prayer at this juncture of growth is the fundamental union which consists in a growing conformity to God's will. "True union can very well be reached, with God's help," she explains, "if we make the effort to obtain it by keeping our wills fixed only on that which is God's will. . . . This union with God's will is the union I have desired all my life; it is the union I ask the Lord for always and the one that is clearest and safest."[9] This union is the result of the inflow of God's love in one's life. The manifestation of this union is a life lived in love of God and love of neighbor.

Teresa's symbol for the transformation of a soul in union with God is also the symbol for all the psychological transformations which take place on the pilgrimage to the center. The development of personality demands the re-enactment, over and over, of the story of the death of the worm and the birth of the butterfly. Our passages, crises, transformations all involve a dying and a rising. Teresa's *The Interior Castle* is the story of one large transformation, one grand passage, one great initiation. The castle itself is the cocoon-container of a death and a new life. Each of the dwelling places marks varieties of transitions and turning points.

One striking message of *The Interior Castle* is the necessity of change in life. It anticipates the findings of modern developmental psychology regarding passages. Teresa makes clear the fact that the adult Christian cannot remain on a plateau. If life is to continue to develop the plateaus will come to an end as the ground shifts. At the shifting point, the cocoon, an upheaval takes place. The process is similar to the action of the large plates forming the surface of the earth. Where they grind together the earth is fractured, mountains are pushed up, and cracks appear. Or it is similar to a quiet river which empties into a whirlpool. Once past the turbulence the river can continue its quiet journey, for a while.

For psychological life to develop, the psyche must die these deaths. And Teresa reminds us that the Christian journey is marked by crosses. Both perspectives are present in *The Interior Castle*. The book presents a spirituality which recognizes human development. At the same time, it offers the challenge of finding Christ's dying and rising within the transformations of consciousness. The butterfly symbolizes the paschal mystery as well as psychic growth.

In the next section I will comment further on the situation of the psyche which is symbolized by the cocoon. From Carl Jung's viewpoint, it is a troubling but rich phase of development.

The Cocoon as Alienation

The challenge in human development, according to Jungian psychology, is to establish a healthy axis of communication between the ego and the self. This relationship is paramount in the development of personality. As a matter of fact, in all archetypal images the ego is meeting at least an aspect of the self. The images we have been studying in *The Interior Castle* are all self-images in one way or another.

Two extremes in the relationship between the ego and the self are perennial experiences of the individual. One extreme is the collapse of the axis of communication and the ego is then identified with the self. This situation is termed inflation. The child begins in the inflated state of ego-self identification. And the adult periodically through life loses touch with the self and begins to live as though the world centered on the adult's consciousness. Edward Edinger, a Jungian analyst, points out the subtle forms of inflation: "Too much humility as well as too much arrogance, too much love and altruism as well as too much power striving and selfishness, are all symptoms of inflation."[10] In other words, when we are taking too much credit or too much blame in life we are probably identifying with the self. One deep-down residue of inflation, Edinger mentions, is the illusion of immortality.

The other extreme in the relationship between the ego and the self is the total rupturing of the axis of communication. This loss of contact with the self is experienced by the ego as deep rejection. Edinger refers to this situation as a time of alienation. One symptom of the alienation is a lack of self-acceptance. When the alienation is so severe that it becomes unendurable it leads to acts of violence against oneself or others. The scriptural image of the first couple being cast out east of Eden symbolizes the experience of the ego separated from the self.

This alienation is the result of a previous inflation, according to the scenario presented by the Jungian Edinger. In an inflated state, with the ego identifying with the self, the individual acts in a way which goes beyond human limits. The over-stepping of boundaries results in disastrous consequences as evidenced in the myth of Icarus whose wax wings melted when he flew too near the sun. The experience of the limitations of life breaks the bonds of inflation and seriously damages the relationship between the ego and self. The individual then moves into the state of alienation.

Slowly, a change takes place in the individual which allows for a re-establishing of a proper relationship with the self. The ego-self axis begins to heal and the personality continues to develop. In time, renewed inflation takes place and the cycle begins again, each time bringing about growth in consciousness. This scenario is especially true in the early stages of life and until a stable relationship can be developed between ego and self.

The above scenario is a helpful way, I believe, for amplifying Teresa's butterfly image. The cocoon is a stage of alienation, necessary but difficult. The voyager through the castle leaves known, secure roads in life and is led into a wilderness where the way is unknown. The wilderness is a land of alienation, as the cocoon is a totally different, dark condition for the silkworm. In this state of alienation, this cocoon, an old way dies and a new way begins. It is the story of all crises and transformations. It is the scenario not only for the fifth dwelling place, where Teresa first uses the butterfly image, but for the entire castle adventure, and the transitions involved in all the dwelling places. From a religious perspective the story includes the invitation to enter into the dying and rising of Christ and so enter into union with God.

In terms of the polarities of the psyche, the symbol of the cocoon may be explained this way. One pole is present in the conscious personality of an individual. It is, therefore, in the light and its opposite is not known to the individual because it dwells in the darkness of the unconscious. The energy of the psyche is in progression and the personality is adapting adequately to the environment. This conscious pole—let us say it is the feeling function—is part of that successful adaptation. But in time that function will no longer be adaptive to all the demands of the outer world, and the other pole, the thinking function, will be required. Because the thinking function has not been recognized by the personality a certain disorientation sets in. The individual is confused and "at sea."

During this time the progression of energy ceases and a regression of energy begins. In other words, energy no longer flows into the conscious function but is now withdrawn from that function so that a better adaptation can be made to the inner world which now seeks expression. In effect, the two sides of the polarity now confront one another as thesis and antithesis. In this clash the poles negate one another and the ego is thoroughly in the dark. It is this situation which is symbolized by the cocoon. The cocoon is the place of darkness and heat and the container of transformation. It represents the "dark interval" which occurs within a person when fundamental worldviews, values, and identity are challenged and broken. The cocoon is the sepulchre of broken images. It is also the incubator supporting living figures.

When the conscious pole meets the unconscious pole the ego is immobilized and the progressive flow of energy is blocked. The libido then regresses into the unconscious and seeks a common ground which will allow for a recognition of the basic unity of the two poles. Entry into the cocoon of tense confusion, and groping for a way out, is a painful process which attends any growth of consciousness. It feels like dying. Jung wrote: "The dread and resistance which every natural human being experiences when it comes to delving too deeply into himself is, at bottom, the fear of the journey to Hades."[11]

The Dark Night of the Soul

Psychologically, the ego experiences alienation as a prelude to meeting the self. This same state of alienation is part of the religious experience of contacting God in one's depths. The religious invitation to union with God exists within the psychological development. As a religious experience this cocoon time of alienation has been called "the dark night of the soul." St. John of the Cross, another Carmelite Spanish mystic and friend of St. Teresa, used the image of night to express the Christian journey in faith. More vividly than Teresa, John's writings emphasized the cocoon phase of transformation through union with God. The dark night stands as symbol of the purifications experienced by the Christian.

Notice how John's instructions for seeking union with God make use of polarities and inevitably lead to a dark experience:

> To reach satisfaction in all
> desire its possession in nothing.
> To come to possess all
> desire the possession of nothing.
> To arrive at being all
> desire to be nothing.
> To come to the knowledge of all
> desire the knowledge of nothing.
> To come to the pleasure you have not
> you must go by a way in which you enjoy not.
> To come to the knowledge you have not
> you must go by a way in which you know not.
> To come to the possession you have not
> you must go by a way in which you possess not.
> To come to be what you are not
> you must go by a way in which you are not.[12]

In terms of the relationship between the ego and the self, these instructions are in praise of the non-inflated ego. And they contain the insight that a true experience of the self is a defeat for the ego.

John's night image has three phases: twilight, midnight, and dawn. Dawn is the time of union with God, but twilight and midnight refer to the night of the senses and the night of the spirit which precede union. The night of the senses is a time of dryness when both the things of God and the things of the world lose their appeal.[13] John's description of this state has a certain correspondence to the situation of individuals in Teresa's third dwelling place who discover they have to move on. It is, after all, a time of twilight, and that which was seen so clearly now becomes blurred. In Jung's psychological framework, the person's conscious attitude is no longer sufficient to provide meaning and the unconscious is stirring and dimming the bright light of consciousness. The ego needs life-giving contact with the self. But first, the ego needs to be dis-identified from the self in order to eventually have a relationship with that self. John likens the experience to being led into a desert solitude. In effect, the many centers where the self was previously located are now giving way to the true center. This process corresponds to the pilgrimage to the center in *The Interior Castle*.

The night of the spirit, midnight in the journey of faith, is a more intense experience still. All support systems are found wanting, and only a naked faith sustains the pilgrim. In the darkness of this cocoon experience the contrast between the polarities is stunning. "The brighter the light," John writes, "the more the owl is blinded."[14] It is as though the plunge into the depths, the movement toward mystery which is at the center, evokes this question: Are these depths, is this center, trustworthy? Is the center for me, sustaining and life-giving? But no answer is given, and the trust itself must become its own reason. John's images for this experience parallel Teresa's cocoon image. He compares the experience to being swallowed by a beast, being tried in a crucible, being in the depths of the sea, being in a sepulcher of dark death, and peering into hell.

If the story of the silkworm's transformation into a butterfly is taken to represent the entire journey to the center in the castle, then the cocoon phase of the story would pertain to the experiences in the fourth, fifth, and sixth dwelling places. Here Teresa experiences the "nights" reported by John of the Cross. These dwelling places describe the effect of the encounter of the large polarity seeking union in the castle, the polarity which is the soul and God. And nowhere is the bittersweet struggle more intense than in the sixth dwelling place. It is the night of the spirit and the trustworthiness of the center is in doubt. Teresa writes: "The Lord, it seems, gives the devil license so that the soul might be tried and even be made to think it is rejected by God. Many are the things that war against it with an interior oppression so keen and unbearable that I don't know what to compare this experience to if not to the oppression of those that suffer in hell, for no consolation is allowed in the midst of this tempest."[15]

Teresa points to some of the sources which caused her pain during this time of her life. She was both ridiculed and praised for her spirituality. Either response by others was a difficulty for her. And her physical health was a continual problem. She writes of herself: "I know a person who cannot truthfully say that from the time the Lord began forty years ago to grant the favor that was mentioned she spent even one day without pains and other kinds of suffering (from lack of bodily health, I mean) and other great trials."[16]

Inexperienced, fearful confessors, without much learning, added to Teresa's confusion. "Everything is immediately condemned as from the devil or melancholy."[17] These outside criticisms simply reinforced her own inner self-criticism: "The soul doesn't think that it has any love of God or that it ever had any, for if it has done some good, or His Majesty has granted it some favor, all of this seems to have been dreamed up or fancied. As for sins, it sees certainly that it has committed them."[18] Her language is straight from the experience of the night of the spirit.

During this time Teresa was also undergoing ecstatic experiences which added to the general unsettledness. They were evidence in her life of the growing union with God. In the description of the sixth dwelling place, the longest description in *The Interior Castle*, Teresa includes a discussion of these ecstatic experiences.

Approaching the Center

The ecstatic experiences are not central to union with God, but they were manifestations of the transformation taking place in Teresa as she approached the time in her life which she would identify as the seventh dwelling place.

Psychologically, the state of alienation, the rupture of any relationship between the ego and the self, can lead to the re-establishment of a true relationship between the two. In this movement, the ego begins to approach the center of the psyche, the self, and the experience of this center can be awesome. Especially after an intense experience of alienation the self is often encountered in a striking manner similar to Moses' experience of the burning bush.

Interestingly, Edward Edinger has made this observation: "When a woman (or the anima in a man's psychology) encounters the Self it is often expressed as celestial impregnating power."[19] Teresa appears to be using such imagery when she tells of an experience in which the soul "feels that it is wounded in the most delightful way. . . . And even if the soul does not want this wound, the wound cannot be avoided. But the soul, in fact, would never want to be deprived of this pain. The wound satisfies it much more than the delightful and painless absorption of the prayer of quiet."[20]

She continues to talk about the experience in paradoxical terms. It is an action of love on God's part which is both painful and delightful. "I do know that it seems this pain reaches to the soul's very depths," she says, "and that when He who wounds it draws out the arrow, it indeed seems in accord with the deep love the soul feels that God is drawing these very depths after Him."[21] The experience of union is not as abiding as it will be in the seventh dwelling place which is the time of the spiritual marriage. This experience of union, in the sixth dwelling place, she terms betrothal.

The experience of approaching the last dwelling place, the center of the castle, is so powerful for Teresa that it disrupts her inner and outer environments. "O God help me," she writes, "what interior and exterior trials the soul suffers before entering the seventh dwelling place!"[22]

The following descriptions are presented for the sake of completeness, and not to distinguish, psychologically, among the experiences.

Among the events of this time, Teresa speaks of hearing locutions.[23] Sometimes these messages seemed to originate from within herself, while at other times the messages came from outside. It seemed, at times, as though she were actually hearing a spoken word. She counsels that the source could be the imagination, the devil, or God. But if they are from God, the words will have power and authority. They will bring peace and will make an impression that will not be forgotten for a long time, sometimes never. She advises not acting on a message until a learned and prudent confessor is consulted. And if the words are from God, they will be fulfilled in any event.

On other occasions, a word which Teresa heard or remembered about God led to an ecstasy, or transport or rapture, all meaning something similar to Teresa. She distinguished ecstasy from union which was not as powerful in its effects nor did it cause phenomena which are associated with ecstasy. In these ecstasies, Teresa had visions about God, some imaginative with actual images, and others simply intellectual, as she called them. With the latter visions there was nothing she could report, but she was left with a deep conviction concerning the grandeur of God.

On these occasions her experiences took on powerful numinosity. She likened them to the experience of Moses and the burning bush. And she also compared them with an experience she had of seeing an impressive room in the Duchess of Alba's house on one occasion. The room was filled with noteworthy objects. But in remembering the occasion, Teresa could not remember the individual items but only her overall impression of the room. Intellectual visions produced just such effects in her. She says, "After it returns to itself, the soul is left with that representation of the grandeurs it saw; but it cannot describe any of them, nor do its natural powers grasp any more than what God wished that it see supernaturally."[24] Physical effects of these ecstasies may include reduced breathing and a lowered body temperature.

Another kind of ecstasy or rapture Teresa calls the "flight of the spirit." She attempts to describe it: "It is such that the spirit truly seems to go forth from the body. On the other hand, it is clear that this person is not dead; at least, he cannot say whether for some moments he was in the body or not. It seems to him that he was entirely in another region different from this in which we live, where there is shown another light so different from earth's light that if he were to spend his whole life trying to imagine that light, along with the other things, he would be unable to do so."[25] She uses the image of a giant snatching up a straw, or a huge wave lifting a tiny bark, to express the experience.

In this "flight of the spirit" Teresa receives imaginative and intellectual visions. She says more is learned in an instant than years of study could produce. In particular, three things are impressed upon the person: "knowledge of the grandeur of God . . . ; self-knowledge and humility . . . ; the third, little esteem of earthly things. . . ."[26]

The result of all these experiences is an increased desire to be one with God. This desire leads to a mixture of wishes: to die and leave this exile; to retreat into the desert, fleeing people who might be the occasion of offending God; to enter more fully into the world in service of God. Women do not have equal opportunities, she notes. "A woman in this stage of prayer is distressed by the natural hindrance there is to her entering the world, and she has great envy of those who have the freedom to cry out and spread the news abroad about who this great God of hosts is."[27]

Two other effects of this prayer are briefly discussed. One is tears which come to a person who so desires God. She recommends hard work and virtue as more practical than weeping. So she advises her sisters to "let the tears come when God sends them and without any effort on our part to induce them. These tears from God will irrigate this dry earth, and they are a great help in producing fruit. The less attention we pay to them the more there are, for they are the water that falls from heaven."[28]

The other effect she discusses is the urge to praise God in an exuberant, but unintelligible, prayer. It appears to be a kind of "gift of tongues." She says that "our Lord sometimes gives the soul feelings of jubilation and a strange prayer it doesn't understand. I am writing about this favor here so that if He grants it to you, you may give Him much praise and know what is taking place. . . . The joy is so excessive the soul wouldn't want to enjoy it alone but wants to tell everyone about it so that they might help this soul praise our Lord. All its activity is directed to this praise."[29]

Throughout this sixth dwelling place Teresa refers to the soul undergoing these experiences as a "little butterfly." She began using the image of a silkworm and its change into a butterfly in the fifth dwelling place as a symbol of transformation which takes place in union with God. Since this union is not stable and complete until the seventh dwelling place, and since the sixth dwelling place contains experiences of the "dark night" including raptures which accompany the transformation, I have been envisioning dwelling places four, five, and six as the cocoon stage of the butterfly story. In the large journey through the castle these dwelling places contain, as in a cocoon, the encounter of the great polarities of the soul and God with the resulting experiences of the "otherness" of God and the simultaneous deep desire for oneness. Here the transformation is still in process and the darkness and confusion are still evident.

The psychological dimension of this transformation is manifest in the numinosity experienced when the ego enters the realm of the self. It enters on holy ground and is quickly aware that it has left its own environment, its natural atmosphere. As a matter of fact, the psychological and physical effects which Teresa reports bring to mind the disturbances which jar a spacecraft when it enters the atmosphere of a planet. The smooth flight through space gives way to reverberations throughout the ship as it contacts the new environment. A period of disturbance and disorientation ensues until an adjustment and a new way of being is attained.

The ego slowly adjusts to a new and nourishing relationship with the self. The experience of alienation and the "dark night" gives way to the dawn of the emerging self. The butterfly is indicative of the healing process that has taken place in the depths of the psyche, a healing which comes from the mystery at the center. The butterfly as emerged from the cocoon is the appropriate symbol for the following discussion of this healing process.

The Butterfly as Symbol of the Healing Process

Within the psyche a power is available to heal the woundedness of alienation and to bring new life out of darkness and disorientation. Where a wall appeared to be blocking any further progress, an opening slowly appears and life's journey can be resumed with lessons learned and hopes renewed. In times requiring conversion and serious readjustment, a healing strength is available which is experienced as a power coming from beyond our own weak condition. This power helps us grow through the crisis time, supporting us as we grieve over and accept what had to die, and opening us to the new possibilities tentatively taking root in the darkness. The butterfly is an apt image for the delicate freeing-up of a condition which had felt like an entombment. It speaks of a fragile lifting-up of a heart which had been heavily weighed down. This healing process has a central place in the psychology of Carl Jung, and his effort to understand and describe this process is one of his major contributions.

In Jung's theory, as we had begun to discuss it, the disorientation came when the conscious attitude was no longer adequate for the demands that life was placing upon it. The ego needed to establish a relationship with the self which would free the ego from its cramped condition. In terms of the polarities of the psyche, the crisis time begins when one pole which was part of the conscious personality is forced to encounter a contrary pole in the unconscious. This contrary pole represents new life and would allow more of the self to come to light. But the two poles apparently negate one another and the ego is caught in the middle. The ego gradually realizes that it participates in both poles, for example thinking *and* feeling. But consciousness has no way of uniting these opposite aspects of psychic life. The will cannot choose either pole and so its activity is suspended. Energy flows from the now neutralized consciousness and regresses into the unconscious bringing about new activity in that realm.

Here is Jung's description of that situation: "All progress having been rendered temporarily impossible by the total division of the will, the libido streams backwards, as it were, to its source. In other words, the neutralization and inactivity of consciousness bring about an activity of the unconscious, where all the differentiated functions have their common, archaic root, and where all contents exist in a state of promiscuity of which the primitive mentality still shows numerous vestiges."[30] Life cannot tolerate the standstill of vital activity. The energy flows to a point below the clash of opposites where they both have a common source. From this common ground a new psychic content emerges, a new attitude develops, which compensates for the division which is being experienced. This new life becomes a middle ground for the meeting of the opposites. The energy of the opposites now begins to flow in one shared direction and a new way of being enlivens the personality. The total psyche, both conscious and unconscious, has played a part in the breakthrough. "I have called this process in its totality," writes Jung, "the *transcendent function*, 'function' being here understood not as a basic function but as a complex function made up of other functions, and 'transcendent' not as denoting a metaphysical quality but merely the fact that this function facilitates a transition from one attitude to another."[31]

The four psychological functions of thinking, feeling, sensing, and intuiting all have a role in the resolution of the problem. Their activity is seen in the new psychic content, the symbol which unites the opposites and heals the psyche. Jung points to this "living symbol": "The raw material shaped by thesis and antithesis, and in the shaping of which the opposites are united, is the living symbol. Its profundity of meaning is inherent in the raw material itself, the very stuff of the psyche, transcending time and dissolution; and its configuration by the opposites ensures its sovereign power over all the psychic functions."[32] Thus the transcendent function refers to the psyche's process of symbol-formation.

Jung stressed the point that a living symbol is the result of the activity of both the unconscious and consciousness. A psychic content which is strictly the creation of the unconscious is no more a symbol than something created consciously. Both contents require attention by an observing consciousness which is open to symbolic meanings. Something created by an artist is not a symbol for that artist if she does not consciously attend to that image with a symbolic attitude. A living symbol requires the participation of both consciousness and the unconscious.

In this collaboration between the known and unknown parts of the psyche the four functions are engaged. The symbol formed in the process will be imagery which the sensation function can perceive. At the same time the symbol will stimulate the intuitive function since it is pregnant with meaning. The symbol invites the reflection of the thinking function as the individual gropes for understanding of the situation. And the image as symbol becomes an expression of the powerful feeling which accompanies the experience. The result of the process of symbol-formation is a new relationship between the conscious and the unconscious parts of the psyche. This transcendent function produces a healing in the psyche. The new symbol, a uniting symbol, signals the relative completion of the passage or transformation from one state of consciousness, through a time of painful readjustment, to a new state of consciousness. The ego is now properly related to the self which is the source of the healing power for the psyche. Their relationship is not one of inflation or alienation but of life-giving communication.

All living symbols are uniting symbols. At the very widest interpretation they unite the known with the unknown. We have been studying the imagery of *The Interior Castle* with the assumption that this archetypal imagery is symbolic and that, consequently, these symbols are uniting symbols. The complete image of the silkworm-cocoon-butterfly is representative of a uniting symbol. The opposites of a lower form and a higher form are kept in unity by this symbol. The circular mandala is a common uniting symbol. The opposites are held together in tension within the whole of the circle. And the image we will look at in the next chapter is a symbol of union frequently used by the mystics: the spiritual marriage.

Teresa approached images, whether they originated within her psyche or in the world around her, with the attitude that they spoke of the unknown as well as the known. She reminds the reader that even in the smallest part of creation there is more than we know. Consequently, it is safe to assume that her imagery contains within it living symbols, formations that are the product of the transcendent function of her psyche. For a reader, the butterfly image may not be a living symbol, because one person's symbol may be just another image to another person. But for Teresa this image very probably expressed experiences of transformation and she uses it to communicate an understanding of the effects of union with God. Most certainly, her experiences of her depths were mediated by numerous other uniting symbols. Her attention to these images, as well as her exhortations to live a symbolic life, points to a healing process within the life of every reader.

Relating to the Unconscious

In a later preface to a paper written in 1916 titled, "The Transcendent Function," Jung poses a central question: "How does one come to terms in practice with the unconscious?" The paper, written during the time in his life when he was absorbed with the task of relating to his own unconscious, discusses certain approaches to this task. Although it is an early paper in his career, it is an extremely significant one since the problem it poses and the procedures it suggests remain foundational to Jungian psychology.[33]

Jung speaks of two steps in the process of coming to terms with the unconscious. The first step requires hearing the unconscious; the second step involves consciousness relating to this content from the unconscious. The two steps help facilitate the process involved in the transcendent function of the psyche.

The first step, hearing the unconscious, requires effort since consciousness usually is dominant and drowns out any other voices. Often it takes a critical problem to arise before consciousness is motivated to listen to the unconscious. Jung discusses several ways of listening to the content of the unconscious. I have already discussed a number of these approaches in the first chapter, but, because of their significance, it will not be amiss to briefly recall them. The purpose of Jung's paper, "The Transcendent Function," is to relate these procedures to the overall process involved in the transcendent function. He does not go into great detail concerning their implementation.

Because he has in mind the context of analysis, Jung cites the analyst as a key mediator of the transcendent function. The analyst helps bring consciousness and the unconscious together in a new relationship. Jung makes the helpful observation that a "cure" is not an appropriate way of speaking about the goal of analysis. "Analytical treatment," he says, "could be described as a readjustment of psychological attitude achieved with the help of the doctor."[34]

As one primary source of unconscious material, Jung mentions dreams. I previously went into some detail concerning Jung's approach to dreams. In this paper he simply says that while they are a relatively pure source of unconscious content, they are difficult and demanding to work with and other sources might prove more helpful.

As another source, Jung speaks of "spontaneous fantasies." With practice, people can relax their conscious control of psychic processes, which Jung terms "eliminating critical attention," and allow fantasies to emerge. In particular, he encourages entering into the mood or the emotional disturbance as a beginning point. Sinking into the mood, the individual can then write down the images and other associations which arise. He says that this procedure enriches the affect, brings the unconscious contents closer to consciousness, and allows for increased understanding of the material expressed in the feelings. This relating to the unconscious through the feelings of the situation is the beginning of the trancendent function.

Another helpful way of entering into affect is to present it in some picture form. To draw or paint feelings which are being experienced is a way of providing a forum for fantasy. In this process not only is the unconscious allowed room for expression but consciousness is given a form to reflect upon. Again, the procedure aids the transcendent function in relating conscious and unconscious aspects of the psyche.

"Often, however," Jung observes, "we find cases where there is no tangible mood or depression at all, but just a general, dull discontent, a feeling of resistance to everything, a sort of boredom or vague disgust, an indefinable but excruciating emptiness. In these cases no definite starting point exists—it would first have to be created."[35] He recommends a restful environment which would aid a process of introversion. The night is a natural time of introversion for the libido. He then recommends:

> Critical attention must be eliminated. Visual types should concentrate on the expectation that an inner image will be produced. As a rule such a fantasy-picture will actually appear—perhaps hypnagogically—and should be carefully observed and noted down in writing. Audio-verbal types usually hear inner words, perhaps mere fragments of apparently meaningless sentences to begin with, which however should be carefully noted down too. Others at such times simply hear their "other" voice. There are, indeed, not a few people who are well aware that they possess a sort of inner critic or judge who immediately comments on everything they say or do. Insane people hear this voice directly as auditory hallucinations. But normal people too, if their inner life is fairly well developed, are able to reproduce this inaudible voice without difficulty, though as it is notoriously irritating and refractory it is almost always repressed. Such persons have little difficulty in procuring the unconscious material and thus laying the foundation of the transcendent function.[36]

I find the above paragraph intriguing in the light of the extraordinary experiences of Teresa of Avila. However else her visions and locutions may be explained, there certainly appears to be a psychological dimension which finds some elucidation in Jung's study of the psyche. In her inner journey, it stands to reason that Teresa would meet the images and voices of the unconscious as they express the wider reality she was entering. "For the unconscious is not this thing or that," writes Jung; "it is the the Unknown as it immediately affects us."[37] From the descriptions in the sixth dwelling place of *The Interior Castle* it is evident that the Unknown, God, powerfully affected the body, psyche, and spirit of the woman, Teresa.

Jung concludes his suggestions for hearing the unconscious with the mention of working with one's hands in plastic materials, expressing the unconscious through bodily movements, and being open to the value of automatic writing. For many, the hands are a medium of expression as they mold, or sculpt, or in some other way create. Dancing and other forms of movement are the most natural expression for others. Jung felt, however, that the movements would have to be written down later, or in some way captured, for reflection. Perhaps the availability of audio-visual equipment today would allow for some possibilities.

Therefore the first step in coming to terms with the unconscious requires that we find some way of hearing the unconscious. The various suggestions involved media through which the unconscious could express itself. The second step of the process, now, involves *relating* to the content of the unconscious. In other words, the known and the unknown are brought together for the formation of a third, the uniting symbol. In the first step of hearing the unconscious, the unconscious led and its content was valued. In the second step of relating to this content the ego leads and it must maintain its equally valuable viewpoint.

Jung gives this example:

The way this can be done is best shown by those cases in which the "other" voice is more or less distinctly heard. For such people it is technically very simple to note down the "other" voice in writing and to answer its statements from the standpoint of the ego. It is exactly as if a dialogue were taking place between two human beings with equal rights, each of whom gives the other credit for a valid argument and considers it worth while to modify the conflicting standpoints by means of thorough comparison and discussion or else to distinguish them clearly from one another. Since the way to agreement seldom stands open, in most cases a long conflict will have to be borne, demanding sacrifices from both sides. Such a rapprochement could just as well take place between patient and analyst, the role of devil's advocate easily falling to the latter.[38]

The inner dialogue of the ego with personified parts of the unconscious can take many forms but Jung's example gets to the heart of the process. The *relationship* is key and each of the partners in the dialogue must have a genuine hearing.

Where there is just an image to be related to and a dialogue is not possible, Jung recommends asking oneself: "How am I affected by this sign?" The most direct and natural response is probably the one most helpful. Even if ideas are not forthcoming, certain wordless but real feelings may be the beginning of a more total response.

The processes Jung described in this foundational paper are examples of active imagination, a term he employed to describe the activity of engaging the images of the unconscious. These images become uniting symbols as the known and the unknown relate through them and the transcendent function moves the psyche into a new consciousness. Jung emphasized that it was serious work and is best facilitated by expert supervision. Most experts, if not all, stress the importance of a relationship to another human being in the work of relating to the unconscious. The relationship to the other person, whether counselor, spiritual director, or friend, can be a container in which the contents of the unconscious can be safely and honestly met. The other person helps to mediate the dialogue, and, consequently, becomes a participant in the healing process.

Concluding Reflections and Suggestions

The silkworm-cocoon-butterfly image used by Teresa in the fifth dwelling place symbolized her experience of union with God. This image of transformation led to a discussion of the healing process in the psyche. It is through a series of healings or transformations that the self gradually emerges.

Evelyn and James Whitehead have provided a particularly helpful description of such transformations when they are experienced as adult crises.[39] Patterns can be found in crises.

The Whiteheads point out that a crisis involves a disorientation. The individual feels that something is being lost, but it is not always clear what exactly is being lost. Normal patterns and understandings of life are being disrupted. They no longer have the power to keep the situation under control. And fear often accompanies the confusion because the individual's survival seems to be at stake.

An example of a person's inability to name the problem in a crisis is found in the situation of a young man whose father had recently died. The young man was obviously in a crisis, and said so, but the exact nature of the crisis was not clear to him. He certainly was mourning his father's death, but he was not certain that his grief for his father was the only cause of his consternation. The meaning of the total experience was not clear to him. He was in the middle of something he could not name.

The Whiteheads warn that people in crisis should not be rushed to premature resolutions of their problems. Support groups should give them time to grieve over whatever is being lost. The process takes time before any clarity enters the picture. This particular young man had a support group which encouraged him to stay with his confusion and to listen in the darkness. While he had no meanings to relate to them, he could tell them about images which spoke to him. A particular song, somehow, seemed related to his situation. He was a musician and so he played and sang the song. He also told his group about dream images which had been sticking in his mind. In particular, the image of a baby had been striking in two dreams.

Through these images and his reflections upon them the

young man listened to his experience and attempted to name his loss. The group supported him in his bereavement. I never learned how long it actually took before this man had some clarity in his situation, but I have always remembered the efforts both he and the support group made to be attentive to the experience of a crisis.

The resolution of such crises requires a letting-go, a receptivity. When the normal controls over life have disappeared, an individual is opened to the possibility of deep learnings. The crisis becomes a religious experience when an invitation from God is discerned at the basis of the crisis. A person of faith believes that God is a supporting, challenging presence in this experience. A letting-go is required so that God can bring about something new in the person's life.

People report that resolutions to their crises are experienced as something which happens to them. When I have asked groups of people to describe their experiences of transformation and conversion, they say that the healing was experienced as a power, a strength coming to them from beyond themselves.

In our discussion, the healing of the division between the human and divine in the experience of union is the large context within which the psyche's healings take place. In Jungian psychology the self is the source of the healing, but that self is essentially a mystery.

Teresa's faith experience allowed her to name the mystery which heals. Speaking specifically about the dark experiences of the sixth dwelling place, she writes: "In sum, there is no remedy in this tempest but to wait for the mercy of God. For at an unexpected time, with one word alone or a chance happening, He so quickly calms the storm that it seems there had not been even as much as a cloud in that soul, and it remains filled with sunlight and much more consolation. And like one who has escaped from a dangerous battle and been victorious, it comes out praising our Lord; for it was He who fought for the victory."[40] Healing which is experienced within the psyche is an expression of the healing love of God drawing the soul into union.

Strangely, Jung made a comment to the effect that a saint could never truly experience the healing power of the psyche.

He maintained that the symbols of religion would block the experience of conflict. No opposites would appear because they would be hidden in the religious symbols which would provide answers for any conflicts which did arise. In a 1939 letter he wrote:

> That is why the transcendent function can be observed only in people who no longer have their original religious conviction, or never had any, and who, in consequence, find themselves directly faced with their unconscious. This was the case with Christ. He was a religious innovator who opposed the traditional religion of his time and his people. Thus he was *extra ecclesiam* and in a state of *nulla salus*. That is why he experienced the transcendent function, whereas a Christian saint could never experience it, since for him no fundamental and total change of attitude would be involved.[41]

I believe that Teresa's testimony challenges Jung's contention. Granted, religion can be lived in such an extrinsic manner that it absolves the individual from having to wrestle with conflicting meanings in life. But Teresa's journey is away from such living to an interiorized faith which opens her to fundamental transformations. As a matter of fact, it could be argued that her religious symbols prepared her for the experience of transformation rather than hindered it.

The images of faith we carry with us help shape our experience. True images of faith are symbols which hold opposites in tension and force us to experience a wider reality. If we think of Scripture images we will have some examples, such as a good samaritan, a banquet for strangers, meals with sinners, the last who are first, and the death which brings life. These images of faith contain conflicting poles within them. Generally, the ego identifies with one of the poles, one side of the image. The other pole represents the unwanted, unaccepted unknown. A person who is open to such images of faith is forced to enter into a dia-

logue with this unknown. And in that dialogue the ground is
prepared for a deep change of heart. Teresa's Christian images
prepared her to be open to transforming experiences on her
journey through the castle.

Even in the lofty stages of prayer described in the last two
dwelling places Teresa warns against abandoning Christian images of faith. The known leads to the unknown. She writes:

> It will also seem to some souls that they cannot think
> about the Passion, or still less about the Blessed Virgin
> and the lives of the saints; the remembrance of both of
> these latter is so very helpful and encouraging. I cannot
> imagine what such souls are thinking of. To be always
> withdrawn from corporeal things and enkindled in
> love is the trait of angelic spirits, not of those who live
> in mortal bodies. It's necessary that we speak to, think
> about, and become the companions of those who, hav-
> ing had a mortal body, accomplished such great feats
> for God. How much more is it necessary not to with-
> draw through one's own efforts from all our good and
> help, which is the most sacred humanity of our Lord
> Jesus Christ.[42]

She does not deny that a person in these dwelling places may be
engaged in a loving relationship with God which does not make
use of images or reflection. But she doubts that this state of
prayer will be a continual condition. She reminds the reader
that life is long and the road difficult and it is wise to walk "continually in an admirable way with Christ, our Lord, in whom
the divine and the human are joined and who is always that person's companion."[43] Even if a person's contemplative prayer is
such that he cannot practice discursive reflection, the life of
Christ remains a nourishing source. "But I say," she writes,
"that a person will not be right if he says he does not dwell on
these mysteries or often have them in mind, especially when the
Catholic Church celebrates them."[44] She demonstrates her symbolic attitude when she reminds the reader that God "wants us
to ask creatures who it is who made them."[45]

NOTES

1. Jung, C.W., IXi, 315.
2. Ibid., V, 372.
3. *Interior Castle*, V, chap. 2, nos. 1, 2.
4. Ibid., V, chap. 2, no. 6.
5. Ibid., V, chap. 2, no. 7.
6. Ibid., V, chap. 1, no. 3.
7. Ibid., V, chap. 1, no. 8.
8. Ibid., V, chap. 1, no. 2.
9. Ibid., V, chap. 3, nos. 3, 5.
10. Edinger, *Ego and Archetype*, p. 15.
11. Jung, C.W., XII, 439.
12. John of the Cross, *Ascent of Mount Carmel* in *The Collected Works of St. John of the Cross*, trans. Kieran Kavanaugh and Otilio Rodriguez (Washington, D.C.: Institute of Carmelite Studies, 1973), Book I, chap. 13, no. 11.
13. John of the Cross, C.W., *The Dark Night*, Book I, chap. 9, no. 2.
14. Ibid., Book II, chap. 5, no. 3.
15. *Interior Castle*, VI, chap. 1, no. 9.
16. Ibid., VI, chap. 1, no. 7.
17. Ibid., VI, chap. 1, no. 8.
18. Ibid., VI, chap. 1, no. 11.
19. Edinger, *Ego and Archetype*, p. 70.
20. *Interior Castle*, VI, chap. 2, no. 2.
21. Ibid., VI, chap. 2, no. 4.
22. Ibid., VI, chap. 1, no. 1.
23. Ibid., VI, chap. 3, nos. 1ff.
24. Ibid., VI, chap. 4, no. 8.
25. Ibid., VI, chap. 5, no. 7.
26. Ibid., VI, chap. 5, no. 10.
27. Ibid., VI, chap. 6, no. 3.
28. Ibid., VI, chap. 6, no. 9.
29. Ibid., VI, chap. 6, no. 10.
30. Jung, C.W., VI, 824.
31. Ibid., 828.
32. Ibid.
33. Ibid., VIII, 131–193.
34. Ibid., 142.
35. Ibid., 169.
36. Ibid., 170.

37. Ibid., prefatory note, p. 68.

38. Ibid., 186.

39. Evelyn Whitehead and James Whitehead, *Christian Life Patterns* (New York: Doubleday and Co., 1979), pp. 53–56.

40. *Interior Castle*, VI, chap. 1, no. 10.

41. *C.G. Jung: Letters*, vol. I, p. 268.

42. *Interior Castle*, VI, chap. 7, no. 6.

43. Ibid., VI, chap. 7, no. 9.

44. Ibid., VI, chap. 7, no. 11.

45. Ibid., VI, chap. 7, no. 9.

CHAPTER SEVEN

The Marriage of Masculine and Feminine

Marriage of the masculine and feminine is an archetypal expression of wholeness. In Jung's psychology it refers to a union of the conscious and unconscious poles of personality. In the Christian spiritual tradition marriage is often a symbol for the wedding of the human and divine. Teresa's inner castle journey ends in a spiritual marriage. The psychic and the spiritual marriages are related. A healing of our relationship with God is normally accompanied by intra-psychic and inter-personal healing.

Masculine and Feminine in Jungian Psychology

Every man has a feminine quality within him and every woman has a masculine quality within her. Jung called the feminine element in man the *anima* and the masculine element in woman the *animus*. The anima and animus are archetypal figures representing two modes of consciousness on the continuum of the psyche. When either the anima or animus is dominant in the conscious personality, the opposite pole acts as an inner personality. This inner personality compensates the outer one and exhibits characteristics lacking in the conscious personality.

The precise nature of the anima and the animus remains elusive. "The animus," Jung wrote, "corresponds to the paternal

Logos just as the anima corresponds to the maternal Eros. But I do not wish or intend to give these two intuitive concepts too specific a definition. I use Eros and Logos merely as conceptual aids to describe the fact that woman's consciousness is characterized more by the connective quality of Eros than by the discrimination and cognition associated with Logos."[1] Because of the elusive nature of the material, Jung was aware that his pioneer work remained provisional. Nevertheless, his concepts were firmly grounded in his observations. "Whatever we have to say about these archetypes, therefore, is either directly verifiable or at least rendered probable by the facts."[2] What has to be kept in mind is that his is a masculine consciousness interpreting the "facts."

The anima is described as that which sees relationships, makes whole, values, and reaches out. The animus refers to the ability to discriminate, focus, differentiate, and define. Jung concluded that the ability to cognitively discriminate or focus was less well-developed in woman. The animus has the quality of focused awareness while the anima represents a diffused awareness. The light of consciousness is associated with the animus. The darkness of the unconscious is associated with the anima.

Generalizations about the differences between men and women are difficult, if not dangerous, because of the sensitiveness of the issues. One can only reflect on personal experience and observations, and then judge whether or not Jung is close to the point, or subtly biased. For example, how would you, the reader, judge the accuracy of the following observations of Jung:

> An inferior consciousness cannot *eo ipso* be ascribed to women; it is merely different from masculine consciousness. But, just as a woman is often clearly conscious of things which a man is still groping for in the dark, so there are naturally fields of experience in a man which, for woman, are still wrapped in the shadows of non-differentiation, chiefly things in which she has little interest. Personal relations are as a rule more

important and interesting to her than objective facts and their inter-connections. The wide fields of commerce, politics, technology, and science, the whole realm of the applied masculine mind, she relegates to the penumbra of consciousness; while, on the other hand, she develops a minute consciousness of personal relationships, the infinite nuances of which usually escape the man entirely.[3]

I can think of examples to prove and disprove Jung's assertions. And because men and women would be mixtures of anima and animus, it is probably difficult to find an individual who is a pure example of either. On the other hand, that there is a difference between men and women, a difference byond biological differences, seems evident to me. And I cannot ascribe it totally to a conditioning by society. After all, the symbols of society which socialize us are themselves creations of the human psyche. To view our differences as rooted, at least in part, in the collective, archetypal depths of the psyche seems to be a sensible and promising investigation. At least this approach sheds some light on the mystery of the sexes. The mystery was captured, for me, in a restaurant scene reported by a newspaper columnist. Seated at a table near the columnist's table was an elderly couple. The woman was straining forward, across the table, and was saying to her husband, "What are you thinking?" And he replied, "Nothing." The columnist wondered how many times that dialogue had been repeated in the lifetime of the couple, and how many times men and women throughout history engaged in that very same conversation. I think Jung would say: she was relating; he was reflecting.

In Jung's theory, the anima and animus, as inner personalities, mediate the depths of the unconscious to the individual. Just as the persona assists the individual consciousness in relating to society, so the anima and animus assist that person in relating to the unknown world of the unconscious. The deeper down the psyche we venture, the more unlike our conscious personalities we find ourselves. The shadow is definitely unlike the conscious personality and it resides chiefly in the personal unconscious. But deeper than that, in the collective unconscious, we are so unlike our conscious personality that we even meet a contrasexual side of our psyche, the anima or animus. To contact one's contrasexual side is to have a doorway to the depths.

The anima or animus helps a person enter a fuller life available beyond particular persona roles. The new life that becomes available, when the masculine or feminine within is related to, is not always appreciated by others. "Society expects," Jung warned, "and indeed must expect, every individual to play the part assigned to him as perfectly as possible, so that a man who is a parson must not only carry out his official functions objectively, but must at all times and in all circumstances play the role of parson in a flawless manner. Society demands this as a kind of surety; each must stand at his post, here a cobbler, there a poet . . . because society is persuaded that only the cobbler who is not a poet can supply workmanlike shoes."[4] But the contrasexual side must be met and related to; otherwise it will act negatively in the unconscious.

The negative animus in a woman surfaces as opinion. It purports to be a reasoning, logical process, but in reality the negative animus expresses itself in opinionated views, and argumentation which is not all that logical. The animus merely passes on collective viewpoints, whether they are from parents, books, churches, or other authoritative sources for conventional wisdom. Jung maintains that an analysis of the opinions would show that they are not thought out at all. They are passed on ready-made. Nevertheless, they are held with determined conviction.

The negative anima within a man results in moodiness and touchiness. The man can be filled with resentment and sentimentality. The poorly developed anima disrupts the man's personality because it represents an unintegrated emotional life. The moodiness and sentimentality could be turned into a finely-honed affective life when the anima becomes an integrated part of the personality.

When a woman relates to a man through her negative animus and a man to a woman through his negative anima, the scene is an archetypal clash of collective forces. The two individuals are merely bystanders. Jung writes:

> ... no man can converse with an animus for five minutes without becoming the victim of his own anima. Anyone who still had enough sense of humour to listen objectively to the ensuing dialogue would be staggered by the vast number of commonplaces, mis-applied truisms, clichés from newspapers and novels, shop-soiled platitudes of every description interspersed with vulgar abuse and brain-splitting lack of logic. It is a dialogue which, irrespective of its participants, is repeated millions and millions of times in all the languages of the world and always remains essentially the same.[5]

Either the man or the woman could initiate the dialogue. If a man is moody and withdrawn, the woman's animus may attack with a sharp remark. Or if a woman offers an irritating opinion, the man's anima may respond with sarcasm. However, if both can take the effort to consciously and honestly express their true feelings, as they understand them, then the *individuals* are talking, and not blind archetypes. A beginning has been made to enlighten a situation.

A particularly debilitating effect of a negative anima or animus is that it stifles the individual's creativity. When a man or woman is considering beginning a creative project or taking a step in a new direction, the neglected inner personality acts as a dissenting voice. It undermines a person's activity by questioning the person's ability or the value of the work. It is a voice which attempts to keep an individual from stepping out of a normal path or engaging new dimensions of life. Jung experienced the debilitating effects of his own anima as she challenged the value of his explorations of the unconscious. In his autobiography he recalled: "What the anima said seemed to me full of a deep cunning. . . . the insinuations of the anima, the mouthpiece of the unconscious, can utterly destroy a man."[6]

These negative effects of the anima and animus are the result of neglect of the inner figures. When they are neglected they draw attention to themselves, to the inner realm, by acting in an autonomous way and negatively impinging upon consciousness. Their real role, when acknowledged as inner personalities and related to, is to facilitate communications between the ego and the collective unconscious. The anima and animus introduce the archetypal inner figures to the ego. Jung's theory is rather abstract here, but the important point is that contact with the contrasexual side of the psyche puts a person in touch with fundamental sources of life. These sources of life are essential to the continued development of the personality. And it is the anima and animus which function as a bridge between a person's conscious life and the unconscious.

The positive animus is a guide for the woman who is on an inner journey. In its true role the contrasexual side of the woman sparks the individuation process. At times in his writings Jung identified the animus as the "soul," or essential inner personality, of the woman, just as the anima was the "soul" of the man. However, Jung's wife and other Jungian writers argued that a woman is already at home in her depths. She is at one with her soul which is feminine. The masculine element, the animus, is not the soul but a bringer of light into the darkness of diffused awareness. The animus brings a power of discrimination and understanding, a focused concentration to the feminine depths. Emma Jung wrote: "With the animus, the emphasis does not lie on mere perception—which as was said has always been woman's gift—but true to the nature of the logos, the stress is on knowledge, and especially on understanding. It is the function of the animus to give the meaning rather than the image."[7]

Irene De Castillejo provides a helpful image of the animus:

I personally like to think of my helpful animus as a torch-bearer: the figure of a man holding aloft his torch to light my way, throwing its beams into dark corners and penetrating the mists which shield the world of half-hidden mystery where, as a woman, I am so very much at home.

In a woman's world of shadows and cosmic truths he makes a pool of light as a focus for her eyes, and as she looks she may say, "Ah yes, that's what I mean," or "Oh no, that's not my truth at all." It is with the help of this torch also that she learns to give form to her ideas. He throws light on the jumble of words hovering beneath the surface of her mind so that she can choose the ones she wants, separates light into the colours of the rainbow for her selection, enables her to see the parts of which her whole is made, to discriminate between this and that. In a word, he enables her to focus.[8]

De Castillejo points out that focusing is not the same as thinking. The animus, she insists, is not to be equated with the thinking function. The animus helps the woman to focus inner meanings.

The positive anima accompanies man into the depths of the unconscious where he is not at home. She aids in the individuation process by revealing sources of life which will nourish the development of the man's personality. She enriches his emotional life and enlarges his capacity for love and relationship. Again, certain Jungians point out that the anima aids the process of feeling and relating. It is not identical with them. Just as a woman can think and reflect but is aided in this process by the animus, so too a man can feel and relate but the anima assists the process. Men and women both think and feel. The role of the anima and animus is to direct these functions.

John Sanford, a Jungian analyst and Episcopalian priest, describes the anima's life-giving role in an evocative manner:

Masculine consciousness has been likened to the sun, and feminine consciousness to the moon. At noon everything is seen in bright outline and one thing is clearly differentiated from another. But no one can stand too much of this hot, bright sun. Without the cool, the

moist, the dark, the landscape soon becomes unbearable, and the earth dries up and will not produce life.
That is the way a man's life becomes without the fertil-
izing influence on him of the feminine. Without a relationship to his inner world, a man can focus, but lacks
imagination; he can pursue goals, but lacks emotion; he
can strive for power, but is unable to be creative because he cannot produce new life out of himself. Only
the fruitful joining of the Yin principle to the Yang
principle can stir up his energies, can prevent his consciousness from becoming sterile, and his masculine
power from drying up.[9]

The contrasexual sides of our personalities are often met in
projections. As a matter of fact, Jung considered "falling-in-
love" a privileged example of mutual projection. Because the anima and animus come from the collective unconscious, they
have a mana-like quality and can be compellingly attractive.
When a man unconsciously projects his feminine side on a woman he may be allured by the image of his own anima. Thinking
that he is relating to the woman, he is, actually, beginning to relate to himself at a deeper level. He is meeting his contrasexual
side through the symbol of the woman.

While a man is born with a primordial image of woman in
his psyche, it is not a specific image but only a readiness. Contact with the feminine in his lifetime provides concrete images
of the anima. The early images, such as mother and sisters, begin to give a specific shape to the anima so that only certain
women later in life will have a "hook" for his projections. Not
just any woman symbolizes the anima for a man. But when the
right image is present, the man experiences a sense of coming
home.

And, of course, the woman also meets the animus in projection. When mutual projection is present, two archetypes are relating. Jung characterized the falling-in-love as a relationship of
the "gods." He commented: "The language of love is of aston-
ishing uniformity, using the well-worn formulas with the ut-

most devotion and fidelity, so that once again the two partners find themselves in a banal collective situation. Yet they live in the illusion that they are related to one another in a most individual way."[10]

It takes time for a conscious, individual relationship to grow from this collective beginning. Day to day reality in marriage will slowly wear through the projections and then the business of owning one's contrasexual side and relating to the other person as an individual becomes the challenge. The vertical relationship to one's depths, the inner marriage, is an important balance for the outer, horizontal relationships of friendship and marriage. Jung warned: "Seldom or never does a marriage develop into an individual relationship smoothly and without crises. There is no birth of consciousness without pain."[11]

When individuals are being projected upon by another, they sense a pressure to live out the archetype for the other. For example, women have been carrying the anima projection of men and often attempt to conform to that image for the man. The problems are multiple. Not only is the man excused from integrating a part of his own psychic life and thereby able to grow in personality, but the woman is not given the space to identify and own her own feminine nature. Nor is she able, then, to relate to her animus for her own development. Jung believed that man would not grow in consciousness until woman did. Once woman rejects the anima projection of man, then man is forced to search for completeness within himself. He must begin the process of an inner marriage. And the woman, freed from the constrictions of the feminine in man, can begin to live into her own feminine personality.

Apparently women suffer projections better than men. They will more readily live out the projection of a man's anima than a man will accept the projection of a woman's animus. When a man is asked to carry the soul of a woman, he feels oppressed. Jung said that when it happened to him he felt as though he were a tomb with the dead weight of a corpse within.[12] Perhaps this reaction shows how ill-at-ease man is in contact with unconscious material.

Relating to the Anima and Animus

The images which convey the anima and animus are uniting symbols which are the result of the transcendent function of the psyche. They unite the known, the ego, to the unknown, the unconscious. Working with the anima and animus involves the procedures discussed in the last chapter: recognition of the unconscious content, and relationship with it.

The first problem is recognition of the unconscious content as it appears in symbolic form. Another human being is usually the most impressive image of the anima or animus. "The shadow can be realized," wrote Jung, "only through a relation to a partner, and anima and animus only through a relation to a partner of the opposite sex, because only in such a relation do their projections become operative."[13] Men and women learning to talk together, to express themselves and to listen carefully, are giving attention to the anima and animus within. In listening to one another they begin to learn the shape of their own inner personality. They give that figure room in their life as they maintain a relationship with another person and allow themselves to be led into further dimensions of their personality.

In dreams and fantasy the anima and animus are figures of the sex opposite the dreamer or the one fantasizing. Anima figures can be a range of feminine types from goddesses of mythology, through everyday friends and relatives, to movie and television performers, or simply mysterious, unknown women. James Hillman writes:

> Since men do live psychologically in a harem, it is useful to get to know one's inner household. We do well to know by what fascination we are bewitched: turned into phallic animal, petrified into immobility, or lured underwater and away from real life. We do well to know whom we are unconsciously following in counsel, where our Cinderella sits in dirt and ashes or Snow White lies in poisoned sleep, what hysterical feminine tricks we play deceivingly on ourselves with affects

and moods, which Muse inspires or Beatrice ignites and which is the true favorite who moves the deepest possibilities of our nature and holds our fate.[14]

The animus appears in a similar multiplicity of figures. Irene de Castillejo writes from her experience as an analyst:

> In trying to contact the animus we tend to think of him as one person, although we know he has a multitude of shapes. He can appear as an old man or as a little boy, a learned scholar or an aviator, a god or a devil, a romantic lover or the prosaic figure who styles himself one's husband. . . . Now, if only we can succeed in splitting the animus up into distinct and separate persons we can deal with him. Then I can kneel and ask a blessing of the priest, befriend the feeble-minded boy, face firmly, but with due respect, the devil and order the mealy-mouthed sycophant out of my house. But woe betide me if I lump them all together, call it the animus, and try to deal with that.[15]

What these analysts are suggesting is that once the figures of the anima and animus are recognized in dreams or fantasy, then the next step is to relate to them. Ignored, they operate to the detriment of the individual. Paid attention to, they become invaluable partners in the process of individuation. In his autobiography Jung speaks about his relationship with an anima figure. He heard this inner personality speak to him through a feminine voice. He recognized it as the voice of one of his women patients. Each night he would write down his fantasies and feelings as though he were writing a letter to the woman within. His expectations were that she would help him understand and integrate this matter from his inner world. This process was difficult at first because he found it hard to reconcile himself to such an uncontrolled part of his personality. When his feelings were welling up, Jung asked his anima to produce an image so that he could peacefully, objectively, meet these images and get hold of them consciously. He did so for decades of his life. In his later years he wrote:

> Today I no longer need these conversations with the anima, for I no longer have such emotions. But if I did have them, I would deal with them in the same way. Today I am directly conscious of the anima's ideas because I have learned to accept the contents of the unconscious and to understand them. I know how I must behave toward the inner images. I can read their meaning directly from my dreams, and therefore no longer need a mediator to communicate them.[16]

A dialogue with the inner figures of the anima and animus gives recognition to both the ego and the contents of the unconscious. When a woman dialogues with her animus, two points of view must be present. First of all, she must be able to articulate where she stands, what she wants, what her values are. In other words the woman must be rooted in a respect for her own feminine nature. Then, the animus may be allowed his point of view, his cautions, his suggestions, his comments. The ensuing dialogue, then, will be a true give-and-take, of speaking and listening, of questions and answers, of challenges and disagreement, of compromise. An ignored animus can only voice general opinions. An animus informed with the viewpoint of the woman can speak with more relevance.

A man, too, will establish a relationship with his anima through dialogue. He can begin by entering into a mood or feelings which have a hold on him, and personify them. When given a chance, most unconscious material will seek expression in a personified form, especially the anima and animus. The dialogue can take place entirely in the mind, but the process may be more effective if written down. This concretizing shows respectful attention to both the ego and the anima, and keeps the dialogue from collapsing into one viewpoint. The written dialogue can be reread and reflected upon. The purpose of these dialogues, this exploration of the unconscious, is to return to a wider consciousness involving more understanding, deeper meaning, and responsible living.

The situation of homosexuality, especially among men, was addressed by Jung in terms of the anima and animus:

> Younger people, who have not yet reached the middle of life (around the age of 35), can bear even the total loss of the anima without injury. The important thing at this stage is for a man to be a man. The growing youth must be able to free himself from the anima fascination of his mother. There are exceptions, notably artists, where the problem often takes a different turn; also homosexuality, which is usually characterized by identity with the anima. In view of the recognized frequency of this phenomenon, its interpretation as a pathological perversion is very dubious. The psychological findings show that it is rather a matter of incomplete detachment from the hermaphroditic archetype, coupled with a distinct resistance to identify with the role of a one-sided sexual being. Such a disposition should not be adjudged negative in all circumstances, in so far as it preserves the archetype of the Original Man, which a one-sided sexual being has, up to a point, lost.
>
> After the middle of life, however, permanent loss of the anima means a diminution of vitality, of flexibility, and of human kindness.[17]

John Sanford identifies different types of homosexuality. In one type, a man finds a self-image in another man. This other man represents dimensions of the self which the individual seeks. The relationship between an older man and a younger man, particularly, may be based on projections of the self. According to Sanford, "For the young man, the Self is carried by the older man, who represents the positive father, power, and the authority of the Self. For the older man, the Self is carried by the youth, who represents son, eros, and the eternally youthful aspect of the Self."[18] In these situations of incomplete masculine development, the person projected upon does not represent the anima or animus, but the androgynous self.

In a second type of homosexuality, a man's ego, for one reason or another, has not been able to make a masculine identification, and the anima plays a dominant role. This ascendancy of the feminine influences relationships since the masculine and feminine polarities will not be met in the heterosexual relationship. "These men may have many positive qualities," says Sanford. "They can be quite sensitive, are often easy to talk with, frequently have a gentle, healing quality, and are given to artistic inclinations. In primitive communities, many shamans were homosexual, and in our own day there are certain individuals with healing gifts who have such a homosexual disposition. On the negative side, they can be peevish, fickle in relationships, and oversensitive, which often makes long-lasting, intimate relationships difficult."[19] For both heterosexual and homosexual individuals the inner marriage of the masculine and feminine remains an essential work for the development of personality. Androgyny is the goal of individuation.

The Spiritual Marriage

The goal of Teresa's spiritual journey is expressed in terms of masculine and feminine. In the seventh dwelling place, Teresa uses a universal image for the union of the human and divine, the spiritual marriage. The close, personal relationship between a man and a woman in marriage is some indication of the nature of the prayer experience in this last dwelling place. The experience of union with God began in the fifth dwelling place, intensified in the sixth dwelling place, and now reaches its goal as the soul continually lives in the center of the castle. Teresa hopes to be able to give some description of this state: "Thus you will understand how important it is for you not to impede your Spouse's celebration of this spiritual marriage with your souls, since this marriage brings so many blessings, as you will see."[20]

Teresa hesitates to write about this deep union with God because she does not want people to think that she is writing from experience, which she is. She was tempted to conclude *The Interior Castle* at this point. But upon further reflection, she decided that it would be neglectful to omit discussing these experiences. She consoled herself with the thought that her writing might not appear until after her death. And so she continued to attempt to describe this prayer.

She struggles with a description of something which cannot be captured in words. She stays with marriage imagery as her best hope of expression: "When our Lord is pleased to have pity on this soul that He has already taken spiritually as His Spouse because of what it suffers and has suffered through its desires, He brings it, before the spiritual marriage is consummated, into His dwelling place, which is this seventh. For just as in heaven so in the soul His Majesty must have a room where He dwells alone. Let us call it another heaven."[21]

Although this union with God began in the fifth dwelling place, it now takes on a different quality. In the fifth dwelling place the union was sporadic, intermittent. In the sixth dwelling place it was ecstatic. Now, in the seventh dwelling place, the union is a peaceful, perpetual condition which Teresa locates at the very center of the soul. This condition is undisturbed by outer events, nor does it manifest itself in any outward manner.

A revelation of the Trinity greets the person who is ushered into the seventh dwelling place:

> When the soul is brought into that dwelling place, the Most Blessed Trinity, all three Persons, through an intellectual vision, is revealed to it through a certain representation of the truth. First there comes an enkindling in the spirit in the manner of a cloud of magnificent splendor; and these Persons are distinct, and through an admirable knowledge the soul understands as a most profound truth that all three persons are one substance and one power and one knowledge and one God alone. It knows in such a way that what we hold by faith, it understands, we can say, through sight—although the sight is not with the bodily eyes nor with the eyes of the soul, because we are not deal-

ing with an imaginative vision. Here all three Persons communicate themselves to it, speak to it, and explain those words of the Lord in the Gospel: that He and the Father and the Holy Spirit will come to dwell with the soul that loves Him and keeps His commandments.[22]

The experience of the indwelling of the Trinity remains with the individual. "Each day this soul becomes more amazed, for these Persons never seem to leave it any more, but it clearly beholds, in the way that was mentioned, that they are within it. In the extreme interior, in some place very deep within itself, the nature of which it doesn't know how to explain, because of a lack of learning, it perceives this divine company."[23] The presence of the Trinity in the soul is not always felt so strongly; otherwise, it would be difficult to give attention to life's demands. But whenever notice is taken, the presence is immediately evident.

Within this experience of oneness with God in the seventh dwelling place, Teresa, more particularly, identifies Christ as the spouse in her experience of the spiritual marriage. She says that the first time the favor was granted, the humanity of Christ was shown to her in an imaginative vision. One day, after receiving Communion, the Lord appeared in majesty and "told her that now it was time that she consider as her own what belonged to Him and that He would take of what was hers. . . ."[24] Teresa here is still predicating the experiences of another person.

This initial experience of a new presence of Christ in the interior of her soul disturbed and frightened her. It was unlike her other experiences in prayer. "You must understand," she explains, "that there is the greatest difference between all the previous visions and those of this dwelling place. Between the spiritual betrothal and the spiritual marriage the difference is as great as that which exists between two who are betrothed and between two who can no longer be separated."[25]

What takes place in the experience of the spiritual marriage is beyond Teresa's power of description. She says that the Lord now appears in the center of the soul in an intellectual vision, no longer in an imaginative way. "What God communicates here to the soul in an instant is a secret so great and a favor so sublime—and the delight the soul experiences so extreme—that I don't know what to compare it to. I can say only that the Lord wishes to reveal for that moment, in a more sublime manner than through any spiritual vision or taste, the glory of heaven. One can say no more—insofar as can be understood—than that the soul, I mean the spirit, is made one with God."[26] Spirit here appears to be the fine point of the soul where God is met.

Teresa takes pains to emphasize the closeness of this union with God. The spiritual betrothal of the sixth dwelling place is a union which does not have the same quality of oneness as the spiritual marriage. She compares the two, speaking first of the union of betrothal:

> Let us say that the union is like the joining of two wax candles to such an extent that the flame coming from them is but one, or that the wick, the flame, and the wax are all one. But afterward one candle can be easily separated from the other and there are two candles; the same holds for the wick. In the spiritual marriage the union is like what we have when rain falls from the sky into a river or fount; all is water, for the rain that fell from heaven cannot be divided or separated from the water of the river. Or it is like what we have when a little stream enters the sea; there is no means of separating the two. Or, like the bright light entering a room through two different windows: although the streams of light are separate when entering the room, they become one.[27]

The oneness with God is such that even the butterfly image is no longer sufficient. The butterfly dies, joyfully, because its life is now Christ. So, the butterfly image dissolves in the seventh dwelling place and it is replaced by the image of the spiritual marriage. It is also replaced by the image of Christ, which will be discussed in the last chapter. All three images, psychologically, are self-images.

While the experience of the spiritual marriage overwhelms Teresa's powers of description, she is able to specify certain effects of the experience. And these effects give a tone to the seventh dwelling place which makes it markedly different from the other dwelling places. As a matter of fact, the seventh dwelling place is a good beginning point for reading *The Interior Castle*. Reading the last dwelling place first may help to offset misguided notions concerning the goal of contemplative prayer. Once the goal is comprehended, then the reader can go back and begin with the first dwelling place.

These, then, are the effects of the spiritual marriage:[28]

First, it engenders forgetfulness of self. The soul does not worry about honor, heaven, or life. She literally trusts that God will look after her, if she looks after what is His.

Second, the soul experiences a great desire to suffer. But the desire is not a compulsion, and if the suffering does not happen she is not upset. The soul "doesn't kill itself as it used to."

Third, the soul experiences a deep interior joy when persecuted, and even has compassion for the persecutors.

Fourth, she desires to serve God by benefiting souls. She is not anxious to die and be with God, as formerly was the case. She wishes to live if God will be praised through her efforts.

Fifth, the soul has a great detachment from everything. She desires either to be alone, or to be doing something which benefits others.

Sixth, in this state she almost never experiences dryness in prayer or inner disturbances as in other dwelling places. "The soul is almost always in quiet." Even the ecstatic experiences practically cease. "Only once in a while are they experienced and then without those transports and that flight of the spirit. They happen very rarely and almost never in public as they very often did before."[29]

The experience of the spiritual marriage is basically inexpressible. But in listing the effects of the marriage Teresa is delineating psychological ramifications of the union with God. These effects give evidence of a personality that has grown into an integrity as a result of the union. The isolated ego of the first dwelling place now gives way to the mystery of the center.

The journey through the castle has resulted in a oneness with God and the emergence of the self. Rather than absorbing the human personality, the union with God has differentiated that personality and given it fullness of life. The inward presence of God has been a guarantee of personhood, not a threat to it.

Not only do the effects of the spiritual marriage give evidence of a wholeness of personality, but the very image of marriage, chosen by Teresa to convey the experience, itself testifies to personal integration. Time and again the human psyche has expressed its rootedness in the ultimate source of meaning through the symbol of marriage. The union of the polarity of the masculine and feminine in marriage has uniquely expressed the deepest unions, the most radical healings experienced by the psyche, including the return to the center and the source of meaning. Consequently, the marriage symbol, precisely because it is a symbol having layers of references, refers not only to the wedding of the human and divine but also to the integration of the conscious and unconscious poles of personality.

The Spiritual Marriage and Androgynous Living

Jung's theory of the anima and animus, the masculine and feminine in the human psyche, suggests the possibility of a rhythm in life. The androgynous person, the person of the inner marriage of the masculine and feminine, is energized by the interplay between the two poles. Alternately active and receptive, the androgynous person flows with life in a give and take, a holding and releasing according to the moment. June Singer, a Jungian analyst who wrote a lengthy study of androgyny, pictures the possibilities: "Without a sense of disjunction, the person will become at once tender and firm, flexible and strong, ambiguous and precise, focused in thinking and diffused in awareness, nurturing and guiding, giving and receiving."[30]

The androgyne is an image symbolizing the union of the two modes of the human personality. The spiritual marriage is an image symbolizing the union of that personality with God. Does the spiritual marriage assume an androgynous person? Does the union of masculine and feminine in the image of the spiritual marriage symbolize not only the wedding of the human and divine, but also the inner marriage of the anima and animus? It would seem so. The pilgrim journeying through the inner castle is entering more deeply into life. The journey is a movement away from the clutches of collective forces and into the reality of one's own psychic life. It is a movement into the unknown, and as the unknown is engaged it slowly reveals itself. Using Jungian categories, the unknown is engaged when the person enters the unconscious, encounters the shadow, and explores the contrasexual side of the psyche. The journey reveals that God is at the center of this life issuing the call to personality. And as that life is more and more centered on, united with, God, the self stands forth in its true completeness and meaning.

Christian tradition usually asserts that the soul is feminine before God. A number of Jungian writers, too, maintain that the soul, the inner personality, of both men and women is feminine. All humans emerge from the nourishing container of the feminine and are forever linked to their ultimate source through the feminine. Women differ from men in their relationship to this matrix. But for both men and women the feminine is the receptive ground for the activity of the divine. The individuation process, the journey into the unknown, allows that feminine pole to be vitally present in the personality.

Carl Jung's pioneer study of the masculine and feminine dimensions within the human personality allows us to amplify the possible psychological meanings symbolized in the image of the spiritual marriage. His concepts certainly do not exhaust the meaning of the symbol, nor do they adequately express the experience of union. But they are the beginning of an effort, from the human side of the equation, to delineate the transformations involved in becoming one with God.

"This is the reason for prayer, my daughers," wrote Teresa, "the purpose of this spiritual marriage: the birth always of good works, good works."[31] Union with God in the center provides a unique view of the world. The spiritual marriage does not take a person from the world, but allows the person to find a place in the essential unity of all creation. The union with God bears fruit in an androgynous living which realizes its intrinsic relationship to all other life and existence. "As it is important to flow with one's natural limitations," writes June Singer, "so is it necessary to flow with one's capacities to think, to plan and to act in the interest of the future. The androgyne participates consciously in the evolutionary process, redesigning the individual, redesigning society, and redesigning the planet, through a process of making ongoing choices."

Singer speaks of two types of choices: hard choices and soft choices. "The *hard choices* are choosing to alter events from the standpoint of ego and power, to alter things to suit one's own wants, and to utilize one's powers to the maximum in order to reach the top." This way is the way of those outside the castle, or in the first dwelling places, who may be building the kingdom of ego consciousness. Singer continues:

> The *soft choice* is the way of the androgyne. This choice comes out of the perspective in which the *individual* (in contrast to the *individualist*) sees himself or herself as only one element in a totality that is ordered by the principle that has been called *Self*, and many other names, but is essentially nameless. The *soft choice* is the choice that comes from being sensitive to the aims of that *Self*, as expressed in the rhythms of nature and the sense of inner harmony that comes from being in tune with them.[32]

This way is the way of the person who lives in the center of the castle and whose responsible living serves the kingdom of God.

The journey culminates in the seventh dwelling place with a clear call to service. Union with God does not preoccupy a person. "You may think," says Teresa, "that as a result the soul will be outside itself and so absorbed that it will be unable to be occupied with anything else. On the contrary, the soul is much more occupied than before with everything pertaining to the service of God, and once its duties are over it remains with that enjoyable company."[33]

Teresa sees no discrepancy in the work of inner and outer

liberation. The inner journey to union with God and outer activity in service of the kingdom are as integral to Christian living as inhaling and exhaling are to breathing. In the seventh dwelling place there could be no question, for example, of having to choose between "spirituality" and "social justice." It would be a false issue. Teresa spells out a fundamental relationship: "I repeat, it is necessary that your foundation consist of more than prayer and contemplation. If you do not strive for the virtues and practice them, you will always be dwarfs."[34] She says that Martha and Mary must be joined. And she points to individuals whose union with God spurred their activity: St. Paul, St. Dominic, and St. Francis. She notes the "hunger which our Father Elijah had for the honor of his God. . . ."[35]

Anticipating her sisters' objections that they have neither the talent nor the scope for great apostolic activity, Teresa advises them to be realistic about their possibilities. They may not be able to benefit the whole world, but they can concentrate on serving those who are nearest them. Do what you can for the love of God, she says. This simple, yet profound, advice concludes *The Interior Castle*. She writes:

> In sum, my Sisters, what I conclude with is that we shouldn't build castles in the air. The Lord doesn't look so much at the greatness of our works as at the love with which they are done. And if we do what we can, His Majesty will enable us each day to do more and more, provided that we do not quickly tire. But during the little while this life lasts—and perhaps it will last a shorter time than each one thinks—let us offer the Lord interiorly and exteriorly the sacrifice we can. His Majesty will join it with that which He offered on the cross to the Father for us. Thus even though our works are small they will have the value our love for Him would have merited had they been great.[36]

Teresa's writing in the seventh dwelling place, as well as throughout the castle, makes it clear that the inner journey to God is also a journey out to our brothers and sisters. I am aware that the contemplative spirituality of Teresa and the psychology of Carl Jung can appear to be disconnected from social responsibility. I hope it has become evident that such a privatized interpretation would be a misreading of both Teresa and Jung. The work of the kingdom takes place in inner and outer realms. Our stress on the individual, inner journey and the contemplative experience is meant to highlight an essential component of Christian living. Christians who labor to change the structures of society realize the importance of this inner work as well. Liberation theologian Gustavo Gutiérrez observes that "modern man's aspirations include not only liberation from *exterior* pressures which prevent his fulfillment as a member of a certain social class, country, or society. He seeks likewise an *interior* liberation, in an individual and intimate dimension; he seeks liberation not only on a social plane but also on a psychological."[37]

John Yungblut, in a conclusion to his book on mysticism, writes:

> I will yield to none in my equally passionate concern for social reform. I was an ardent participant in the revolutionary movement for civil rights as long as it remained committed to nonviolence and integration under the inspired leadership of Martin Luther King, Jr. I have long been a Christian pacifist by conviction. I aspire to remain loyal to the Gandhian principles applied to all forms of direct social action. At the same time, I believe the greatest single need of the church is currently to acknowledge the authentic continuity of Christian mysticism and to accord it the place of pre-eminence it has always deserved and never been granted. Since sound mysticism is itself the primary source of the deepest compassion, wise and sacrificial involvement in movements for revolutionary social reform will inevitably follow for those who identify with it.[38]

Attention to human interiority is not inimical to social activity. Teresa's contemplative spirituality will not lessen a Christian's social awareness. On the contrary, the view from the center of Teresa's castle is much more world-embracing than the ego-constricted view from the periphery. The journey through the castle will result in more, not less, social interest and activity, always, of course, in accord with one's possibilities in life.

Concluding Reflections and Suggestions

The spiritual marriage is an archetypal image symbolizing the goal of our human longing for union with the "other": the other within ourselves, the other human being, the ultimate other who is divine. The psyche consistently expresses otherness in terms of the relationship between man and woman, the masculine and the feminine. Their dialogue effects transformation.

But the feminine is not an equal partner in the dialogue of life today. The Catholic Church, not unlike the larger society, reflects an ambivalence toward the feminine. On the one hand it exalts the feminine, particularly in its devotion to the Virgin Mary;[39] on the other hand, it mistrusts, is suspicious of, perhaps even fears, the feminine as is evidenced by the absence of women in Church leadership.

When women are absent from certain arenas of Church life, the feminine is represented by the anima of the men who are present. That anima is the function of an archetype which is notoriously ambiguous. That archetype can be powerfully positive, or it can be powerfully negative. It produces an attitude in men which may be highly idealistic: "Women! God love them!"; or fearfully pessimistic: "Women! God help us!" When women are present to the men, they provide a concrete imaging of the anima and allow the men to enter into a relationship with the feminine in life. The extreme attitudes toward the feminine may give way to a more realistic, attentive attitude.

Erich Neumann, in his study of the feminine archetype, identifies two characters of the feminine: the elementary and the transforming.[40] It is my impression that the Church is highly endowed with the elementary character of the feminine. The elementary feminine gives birth, nourishes, and surrounds. It manifests a conservative tendency causing it to hold fast to what has been produced. "Mother Church" is an expression of the elementary character of the feminine.

The transforming character of the feminine represents a dynamic element of the psyche which drives toward motion and change. It is this character of the feminine which, I believe, is scarce in the Church when women, and the experience they represent, are not present in important areas of Church life. A matriarchal, elementary, feminine presence is tolerated and even encouraged. But an anima, transformative, feminine presence is discouraged. The elementary feminine nourishes, makes secure, and asks only for loyalty. The transforming feminine demands relationship, risk, and growth.

The growth of the individual requires that the inner masculine or feminine figure be acknowledged, met, and related to in genuine dialogue. The growth of the Church as a human community depends on the essential relationship of the masculine and the feminine. Men and women need to acknowledge the presence of one another. And then we need to enter into genuine relationships where we learn to speak honestly and listen attentively.

NOTES

1. Jung, C.W., IXii, 29.
2. Jung, C.W., IXii, 27.
3. Jung, C.W., VII, 330.
4. Jung, C.W., VII, 305.
5. Jung, C.W., IXii, 29.
6. Jung, *Memories*, p. 187.
7. Emma Jung, *Animus and Anima* (Zurich: Spring Publications, 1957), p. 26.
8. Irene de Castillejo, *Knowing Woman* (New York: Harper and Row, Publishers, 1973), p. 76.
9. John Sanford, *The Invisible Partners* (New York: Paulist Press, 1980), p. 66.
10. Jung, C.W. IXii, 30.
11. Jung, C.W., XVII, 331.
12. Jung, *Visions*, vol. 2, p. 493.

13. Jung, C.W., IXii, 42.
14. Hillman, *Insearch*, p. 101.
15. de Castillejo, *Knowing Woman*, pp. 74, 75.
16. Jung, *Memories*, p. 188.
17. Jung, C.W., IXi, 146, 147.
18. Sanford, *The Invisible Partners*, pp. 95, 96.
19. Ibid., p. 99.
20. *Interior Castle*, VII, chap. 1, no. 2.
21. Ibid., VII, chap. 1, no. 3.
22. Ibid., VII, chap. 1, no. 6.
23. Ibid., VII, chap. 1, no. 7.
24. Ibid., VII, chap. 2, no. 1.
25. Ibid., VII, chap. 2, no. 2.
26. Ibid., VII, chap. 2, no. 3.
27. Ibid., VII, chap. 2, no. 4.
28. Ibid., VII, chap. 3, nos. 1ff.
29. Ibid., VII, chap. 3, no. 12.
30. June Singer, *Androgyny* (New York: Anchor Press/Doubleday, 1976), p. 277.
31. *Interior Castle*, VII, chap. 4, no. 6.
32. Singer, *Androgyny*, pp. 333, 334.
33. *Interior Castle*, VII, chap. 1, no. 8.
34. Ibid., VII, chap. 4, no. 9.
35. Ibid., VII, chap. 4, no. 11. Teresa is alluding to Elijah's statement in 1 Kings 19:10. These words are the motto on the Carmelite shield: *Zelo zelatus sum pro Domino Deo exercituum* ("I have been most zealous for the Lord, the God of hosts").
36. Ibid., VII, chap. 4, no. 15.
37. Gustavo Gutiérrez, *A Theology of Liberation* (Maryknoll, New York: Orbis Books, 1973), p. 30.
38. John Yungblut, *Discovering God Within* (Philadelphia: Westminster Press, 1979), pp. 193, 194.
39. Jung found in the dogma of the Assumption a psychologically significant recognition of the presence of the feminine in a masculine Godhead. He considered the declaration of the dogma as "the most important religious event since the Reformation." C.W., XI, 752.
40. Erich Neumann, *The Great Mother* (Princeton University Press, 1963), pp. 24ff.

CHAPTER EIGHT

Christ, Symbol of the Self

The final image for discussion is the image of Christ. To speak of Christ as an image is not to deny his historicity or his divine-human reality. Accepting these truths, Christ as image is also the symbolic representation of certain meanings for the human personality. The figure of Christ points not only to the historical Jesus and the resurrected God-man but also to the inner life and goals of all men and women.

Carl Jung spoke of a God-archetype within the psyche. The psyche has an affinity for God, a faculty for relationship with God. "This correspondence is, in psychological terms, the archetype of the God-image."[1] But the psychological reality of the God-archetype does not necessarily prove the existence of God. Jung realized that the religious point of view and the scientific point of view approached the God-archetype from different perspectives. "The religious point of view, understandably enough, puts the accent on the imprinter, whereas scientific psychology emphasizes the *typos*, the imprint—the only thing it can understand. The religious point of view understands the imprint as the working of an imprinter; the scientific point of view understands it as the symbol of an unknown and incomprehensible content."[2]

In referring to a God-archetype Jung is saying that the psychological reality which wields the greatest power in the psyche functions as a god. "It is always the overwhelming psychic factor that is called 'God'."[3] But because the referent of this God-archetype is "unknown and incomprehensible" Jung gave it the psychological name of the "self"—"a term on the one hand definite enough to convey the essence of human wholeness and on the other hand indefinite enough to express the indescribable and indeterminable nature of this wholeness."[4]

Consequently images of God are also images of the self. Jung found that, psychologically, "the self cannot be distinguished from an archetypal God-image."[5] The relationship of the God-image to the self is such that "the destruction of the God-image is followed by the annulment of the human personality."[6]

Christ, then, who is image of God, also psychologically refers to the self. He is a divine image and at the same time a self-symbol. Jung stated: "The Christ-symbol is of the greatest importance for psychology in so far as it is perhaps the most highly developed and differentiated symbol of the self, apart from the figure of Buddha."[7] From the account of his life and the pronouncements concerning Christ, Jung was convinced that Christ is the still living myth of our culture. Jung noted the Scripture descriptions of Christ: "He is in us and we in him. His kingdom is the pearl of great price, the treasure buried in the field, the grain of mustard seed which will become a great tree, and the heavenly city. As Christ is in us, so also is his heavenly kingdom. These few, familiar references should be sufficient to make the psychological position of the Christ symbol quite clear. *Christ exemplifies the archetype of the self.*"[8]

Jung is careful to say that he is simply drawing a psychological parallel between Christ and the self. He is not presuming to intrude in the realm of faith. Nor does he think that Christians should be defensive about his approach. "The images of God and Christ which man's religious fantasy projects cannot avoid being anthropomorphic and are admitted to be so; hence they are capable of psychological elucidation like any other symbols."[9]

The implications of Jung's statements about Christ are challenging. As a symbol of the self, Christ addresses the self in men and women. The wider life available to us, but unknown to our ego-consciousness, finds its statement in Christ. He bears our unlived life and yet, often, we fail to recognize that his story is also our story. We give our fuller life away in projections and feel poorly about the narrow life we live. To reflect on the psychological base of the Christ symbol is not to elude Christian mystery but to illumine the conditions which promise greater life. To allow Christ to put us back in touch with our self can be the outcome of such reflection. Teresa of Avila experienced and taught that giving oneself to Christ results in Christ giving us back our self, our self-for-God. She was well aware of an inner faculty of relationship with God, which Jung termed the God-archetype.

Teresa and Christ

As the journey to the center of the castle progresses, in *The Interior Castle*, Teresa more frequently refers to Christ. The development of a relationship with God naturally heightens one's consciousness of Christ. She writes: "For you to see, Sisters, that what I have told you is true and that the further a soul advances the more it is accompanied by the good Jesus, we will do well to discuss how, when His Majesty desires, we cannot do otherwise than walk always with Him."[10]

In a striking manner, Christ became more manifest to Teresa through visions in the sixth and seventh dwelling places. In the sixth dwelling place she speaks of receiving intellectual visions of Christ: "It will happen while the soul is heedless of any thought about such a favor being granted to it, and though it never had a thought that it deserved this vision, that it will feel Jesus Christ, our Lord, beside it. Yet, it doesn't see Him, neither with the eyes of the body nor with those of the soul."[11] Teresa felt that Christ was walking with her on her right side. She was convinced of the reality of the visions when one time she heard the Lord say: "Do not be afraid; it is I."

Teresa also experienced imaginative visions, as she termed them, in the sixth dwelling place. She believed these visions of the Lord to be more beneficial since imaginative visions "are in greater conformity with our nature." These visions represent the Lord in a manner which engages the imagination of the individual.

She writes: "When our Lord is pleased to give more delight to this soul, He shows it clearly His most sacred humanity in the way He desires; either as He was when He went about in the world or as He is after His resurrection. And even though the vision happens so quickly that we could compare it to a streak of lightning, this most glorious image remains so engraved on the imagination that I think it would be impossible to erase it until it is seen by the soul in that place where it will be enjoyed without end."[12]

Teresa explains that this image is not merely a painting but it is truly alive. However, it is not seen with her physical sight. "It is the inner eye that sees all of this."[13] She says that she has never seen a vision with her exterior sense of sight. This inner vision, an alive image of the Lord, had a particular brilliance which she compares to the light of the sun shining through a diamond-like cover.

Teresa distinguishes these visions from images which are produced solely by the individual's imagination. She says that some individuals are so imaginative that they "see" everything they think about. But it is their own imagination which is composing the pictures. They would know a real vision through its suddenness and its stirring effects.

Without again going into Jung's view of the psychological significance of Christ for the human personality, it should be pointed out that Teresa's descriptions of her visions of Christ more than hint at the deeply symbolic nature of these images. Certain images that we have been studying in *The Interior Castle* are symbolic because of the symbolic attitude of Teresa. Other images are symbolic because they are spontaneous, autonomous, productions of the psyche. Examples of the former are water and butterfly; examples of the latter are castle and Christ. However else her visions of Christ may be explained, or wherever else they have their origin, it is evident that they are also products of the symbol-formation process of the psyche.

While these images of Christ are not constructs of the imagination at the conscious level of psychic life, and Teresa mentions that fact, they do give indication of being spontaneous images from the unconscious depths of the psyche. Teresa's description of them as living images erupting into her consciousness is a description of symbolic psychic activity. Again, apart from their origin beyond the individual, and Teresa certainly attributes the visions to God, the psyche is certainly expressing itself through the image of Christ.

Teresa roots the possible sources of her visions in God, the imagination, or the devil. I believe that our psychological understanding of her images points to their source in God *and* the imagination. God is known through the mediation of the psyche. The psyche's images symbolize its experience of God. The devil becomes the apt symbol of psychic life which the individual needs to meet and integrate in an acceptable manner; otherwise, this dark content of the psyche is destructive of life within and outside the personality.

We will further consider the psychological significance of Christ after we finish noting Teresa's references to Christ in *The Interior Castle.*

She follows her description of the imaginative visions of Christ, in the sixth dwelling place, with a discussion of their possible source in the devil. Teresa again gives evidence of her symbolic attitude when she says that any inner or outer image of Christ should be reverenced. "Even though a painter may be a very poor one," she writes, "a person shouldn't on that account fail to reverence the image he makes if it is a painting of our every Good."[14]

In the seventh dwelling place, that of the spiritual marriage, Teresa again speaks of receiving imaginative and intellectual visions of Christ. But they are different from the visions of the sixth dwelling place which is the time of spiritual betrothal. Visions accompanying the spiritual marriage are unlike any others. "You must understand," she writes, "that there is the greatest difference between all the previous visions and those of this dwelling place."[15]

In describing the spiritual marriage she reports: "The first time the favor is granted, His Majesty desires to show Himself to the soul through an imaginative vision of His most sacred humanity so that the soul will understand and not be ignorant of receiving this sovereign gift."[16] Teresa experienced this vision after communion one day. It was a vision of Christ "in the form of shining splendor, beauty, and majesty, as He was after His resurrection. . . ."[17]

The initial experience of the spiritual marriage involves, for Teresa, an imaginative vision of the humanity of Christ. But later experiences find a different presence of Christ, an intellectual vision. Teresa writes, "The Lord appears in this center of the soul, not in an imaginative vision but in an intellectual one. . . ."[18] What is communicated to her, and the delight of the experience, are such that no comparisons can be made.

The result of the spiritual marriage is an identification with Christ. The soul, she says, dies "because its life is now Christ."[19] The passing of time will show the effects of this Christ-life.

The purpose of the Lord's favors in life is not solely for the delight of the soul. "His Majesty couldn't grant us a greater favor than to give us a life that would be an imitation of the life His beloved Son lived. Thus I hold for certain that these favors are meant to fortify our weakness, as I have said here at times, that we may be able to imitate Him in His great sufferings."[20] Teresa observes that those who were closest to Christ, such as his mother and the apostles, suffered the greatest trials.

And when Teresa insists that the spiritual marriage must result in service she says: "Keep in mind that I could not exaggerate the importance of this. Fix your eyes on the Crucified and everything will become small for you. If His Majesty showed us His love by means of such works and frightful torments, how is it that you want to please Him only with words?"[21]

In sum, Teresa tells us that Christ accompanies our journey. Christ is our true life, our final goal. He is the model whom we are to imitate. That imitation will principally be in his suffering. "Fix your eyes on the Crucified. . . ."

A Dark Side of the Christ Symbol

Jung, however, had reservations about Christ as a symbol of the self. Since the self is defined as the psychic totality of the individual, and since the self is never a completed project but always an objective of an ongoing process, symbols of the self do not always represent that self in all its aspects. In the case of Christ as a self symbol, the shadow side of the psyche is missing. Jung stated that "the Christ-figure is not a totality, for it lacks the nocturnal side of the psyche's nature, the darkness of the spirit, and is also without sin."[22] Jung questioned the possibility of wholeness when evil is not part of the mixture.

The appreciation of Christ as a symbol of the self, and yet the regret that Christ is an incomplete symbol, surfaced frequently as Jung struggled with the relationship of religion and the psyche. He firmly believed that the dogmas of religion expressed the realities of the psyche in its development. "Nevertheless," he wrote, "the Christ-symbol lacks wholeness in the modern psychological sense, since it does not include the dark side of things but specifically excludes it in the form of a Luciferian opponent."[23] Every psyche has a shadow, but if Christ is presented as totally in the light, how can the human psyche fully respond to this symbol? Where is the instinctual, earthy, feminine, dark side of Christ? All of these elements are included at one time or another in Jung's portrait of the neglected shadow side of the God-image.

One of the problems, Jung believed, is that Christians view evil merely as the absence of good. While theologically this *privatio boni* doctrine which regards evil as a privation may make sense, psychologically the doctrine does not do justice to the reality of evil as experienced in life. Jung wrote: "Thanks to the doctrine of the *privatio boni*, wholeness seemed guaranteed in the figure of Christ. One must, however, take evil rather more substantially when one meets it on the plane of empirical psychology."[24]

Since psychological development depends upon the struggle and interplay of polarities in the psyche, both good and evil must be present. Psychologically, Jung views good and evil as feeling assessments which are human value judgments. "They are a logically equivalent pair of opposites and, as such, the *sine qua non* of all acts of cognition. From the empirical standpoint we cannot say more than this."[25]

Christians, and particularly theologians,[26] have difficulty with Jung's perception of good and evil as equivalent contraries, especially since he then finds it necessary to place evil within Christ and within the Godhead. He maintains that good and evil, as equivalent poles, must be present together. Theologians have argued that the traditional understandings of good and evil deny his conclusions and, at the same time, make a great deal of sense as assessments within Jung's individuation process.

Traditionally, theological reflection has viewed good as synonymous with completeness. Evil is a subtraction from that completeness. It is a privation, a lack, an absence of something which should be present. In this understanding, good and evil are contradictories, not equivalent contraries. They do not necessarily require one another. Good may be present and acknowledged without any reference to evil. This good, or completeness, is predicated of God.

Jung's individuation process provides a context for the assessment of good and evil as traditionally understood. To be involved in the individuation process is to be moving toward a psychic totality, a completeness called the self. The presence of this self is judged good. Not to be involved in the individuation process results in an absence, a lack of self-knowledge which is properly understood as evil. From this lack of consciousness flow actions and effects which themselves are evil. The evil of not going on the individuation journey is a privation, an absence of self, but it is also the destructive reality which Jung observed in his psychology.

With this understanding of evil, Christ becomes a more adequate symbol of the self precisely because evil is precluded. He represents the goal, the completeness, the good of life's journey. He attracts the self in men and women, opening them to their deepest longings.

But it is understandable that Jung found Christ to be an inadequate symbol of the self. Much of the problem lies with the remoteness of Christ to contemporary Christians. Many Christians experience Christ as one distant from and far above their normal existence. It is difficult for them to reconcile the Christ who is presented in such light with their experience of life lived in a struggle with darkness. Jung was sensitive to life as a struggle between light and dark forces. He believed that religion often avoided the nocturnal side of life, the shadow symbolized by the body, earth, and the feminine. The Church cast off this neglected side of life onto the "Luciferian opponent."

The Crucified Christ

I do think there is an image of Christ available which unites the Christ figure with the shadow, the "Luciferian opponent." It is the image of the crucified Christ. The total image of Christ on the cross, I believe, effectively contains the paradox that Jung felt was being shunned.

It is to just this image of Christ that Teresa calls our attention. "Fix your eyes on the Crucified and everything will become small for you."[27] The imitation of Christ that is the effect of union is an imitation "in His great sufferings."[28] This image in a wordless way makes room for all the serpents within and without the castle. Evil is present and yet transformed in the symbol of the crucified.

The power of this image did not escape Jung. He saw both Christ and the Anti-Christ represented in the scene of the crucifixion: "Both are Christian symbols, and they have the same meaning as the image of the Saviour crucified between two thieves. This great symbol tells us that the progressive development and differentiation of consciousness leads to an ever more menacing awareness of the conflict and involves nothing less than a crucifixion of the ego, its agonizing suspension between irreconcilable opposites."[29]

It would appear that even without the thieves the crucified Christ is a symbol sufficiently evoking the dark powers of life. The shadows have been entered into, not shunned, and the great irreconcilables of life are stretching the figure taut. The human psyche can fully recognize itself in the image. The psyche's individuation process was termed by Jung "a passion of the ego."[30]

Not only is the ego imaged in the crucifixion, but the self as well. Edward Edinger comments on the symbolism of the cross: "Psychologically this means that the ego and the Self are simultaneously crucified. The Self suffers nailing and suspension (a kind of dismemberment) in order to achieve temporal realization. In order to appear in the spatio-temporal world it must submit to particularization or incarnation in the finite. . . . For the ego, on the other hand, crucifixion is a paralyzing suspension between opposites."[31]

One who has reflected in depth upon the crucifixion through Jung's categories is Sebastian Moore in *The Crucified Jesus Is No Stranger*. Moore writes that the initial crucifixion in one's life is a crucifixion of the self. "Only the self, God's self, the self-for-God, is crucified and only by the ego."[32] The ego generally feels that it is being crucified, but in reality it is the self being crucified by the ego.

Moore's analysis of our human situation is that we experience a generic guilt when the ego begins to break away from the initial state of being unconscious. "Guilt, then, is the accusation that freedom draws from the psychic womb whence it breaks out. It grows with consciousness itself. More accurately, it grows with self-consciousness."[33]

The ego senses its isolated and tenuous existence but unconsciously denies this finite, creaturely situation. Cut off from its roots, the ego is forced to find its center in itself. It is suspicious and fearful of any center that asks it to give up its autonomy. The ego acts then in a way which strengthens its autonomy and actually heightens its isolation from the deeper self including life around the ego. Moore writes: ". . . evil consists in an infinite variety of alienation between the conscious ego of man and a total self in which he has his place in God's world. And so, generically, salvation consists in the overcoming of this protean alienation."[34]

The ego, then, crucifies its wider life, the self, in its determined control. We can see why Jung would relate sin to a refusal to come to consciousness. The lack of consciousness, awareness, causes a continuing isolation of the ego with its attendant sinful actions which fix it in place. The self is a threat to this secure existence. It demands a fearful letting-go. When the choice comes, the ego sacrifices the self rather than its own safety. "The crucifixion of Jesus," writes Moore, "then becomes the central drama of man's refusal of his true self."[35] A new title for Jesus is emerging, he maintains, and that title is the "self."[36]

The eventual recognition that the ego is crucifying the self allows the ego to then identify with the self and experience crucifixion in its turn.

Moore provides a helpful illustration from his own life showing how he arrived at an acknowledgement of the crucified self. He had been teaching a course and was quite pleased with it. When asked how the course was going, he responded that it was going well. But the questioner told him that students reported being confused and not satisfied. Moore became despondent.

In a moment of insight he realized that *he* was feeling crucified by the situation, but that in reality he was crucifying the self, the larger life seeking expression in his students and his work with them. "Meanwhile life is trying to breathe," he writes. "This student has understood. That one has not. That other one thinks he has, and has understood something else. And so on. But the ego will have none of this. And its first target—though not easily spotted—is my self, my body, the actual communications that are going out to those men and women."[37]

This insight allowed him to identify with the deeper life being crucified, and that identification became a crucifixion for the ego. The ego-illusions had to give way. The ego was freed from having to worship itself.

Christ on the cross represents the greater life that is the potential of the self. And, Moore insists, that identity is not related simply to an archetype but is an historical person nailed to a cross. He writes: "At every stage of my personal entry into the mystery, the Christ that I have *not* yet become is a man who somehow *is* and not a platonic anthropos-image. This tension seems to be essential to the encounter. Resolve it by dissolving the thought of the Jesus who actually was on that cross, and the encounter itself, with all its power to evoke in me the self, falls to pieces."[38]

In a final reference to Sebastian Moore's stimulating writing I would note a "mystic exercise" which he suggests:

> Now if I am asked to name a mystic exercise in which the ego would have full scope, I cannot think of a more dramatic example than the contemplation of Jesus crucified. For in that contemplation my ego becomes conscious of itself as the crucifier. It is no serene paradigm of human wholeness that is placed before me for my dreamy meditation, but the victim of the way I live. Mysterious though it is and has to be, the process whereby a person enters more and more into life as a necessary and forgiven crucifier of life, answers, to an incomparable degree, to the requirement of depth-psychology: that the ego undergo transformation yet maintain its proper vigour.[39]

It is the exact same "mystic exercise" which Teresa urges in the final dwelling place of *The Interior Castle:* "Fix your eyes on the Crucified. . . ." Teresa's journey through the castle teaches us that the center of the soul may be trusted and we need not continue our ego-isolation in fear of losing everything. The center reveals itself as life-giving, not annihilating. She has gone ahead of us in trusting that the ultimate in life is for her and not against her. But she points not to her life but to the image of the crucified Christ as the symbol that contains *our* life.

The Imitation of Christ

As we have noted, Teresa stresses the importance of the imitation of Christ: "His Majesty couldn't grant us a greater favor than to give us a life that would be an imitation of the life His beloved Son lived. Thus I hold for certain that these favors are meant to fortify our weakness, as I have said here at times, that we may be able to imitate Him in His great sufferings."[40]

The imitation of Christ, for Jung, was no formalistic, external veneration of an ideal. As an external object of worship only, Christ remains distant and unattainable. An imitation of him can become a superficial copying. Jung insists that Christ relates to the outer and inner man, but such an understanding has been weakened in the Church where Christ's relationship to an inner life is often obscured.

He is careful in his criticism: "I am speaking . . . not of the deepest and best understanding of Christianity but of the superficialities and disastrous misunderstandings that are plain for all to see. The demand made by the *imitatio Christi*—that we should follow the ideal and seek to become like it—ought logically to have the result of developing and exalting the inner man."[41]

The imitation of Christ, in Jung's estimation, means that we are to live our individual lives as fully, as responsibly, as authentically as Christ lived his life. We are to enter into our individual existences with the same obedience and integrity which characterized Christ's life.

When Christ remains outside us as an example of the ideal, "man remains fragmentary and untouched in the deepest part of him. Christ can indeed be imitated even to the point of stigmatization without the imitator coming anywhere near the ideal or its meaning. For it is not a question of an imitation that leaves a man unchanged and makes him into a mere artifact, but of realizing the ideal on one's own account—*Deo concedente*—in one's own individual life."[42]

The imitation of Christ is the work of the individuation process. And since the self that comes to be in the individuation process is indistinguishable from the God-image, self-realization in religious terms is imaged in God's incarnation. Individuation is an heroic endeavor involving suffering which Jung called a passion of the ego. The Christ-symbol teaches us the real meaning of individuation. "The drama of the archetypal life of Christ describes in symbolic images the events in the conscious life—as well as in the life that transcends consciousness—of a man who has been transformed by his higher destiny."[43]

Christ is related to the individuation process in the psyches of contemporary men and women because of the pivotal role that the historical Jesus played in the development of human consciousness. Christ represented a significant breakthrough in the slow growth of consciousness in humanity. His life, death, and the experience of his resurrection made that breakthrough attainable for his followers. This viewpoint is carefully presented by William Thompson in *Christ and Consciousness,* and his discussion provides a broad framework for our study of the Christ-symbol and its meaning for the human personality. Because of its relevance, the following material is a brief summarization of certain central points in Thompson's work.[44]

The development of consciousness can be viewed as occurring in broad historical phases. The earliest phase, termed "preconventional," was characterized by a consciousness which was not able to distinguish the person from the surrounding world. People lived in a state of immediacy and participation with nature. They identified with nature which they experienced as numinous and sacred. Their mode of thought is termed "mythical thinking." Although Thompson prefers not to use the category of the unconscious, in Jungian terms this pre-conventional phase was dominated by the unconscious and people experienced themselves totally in projection on the environment.

The "conventional" phase of development followed. It was a transitional phase which coincided with the rise of cities and the great urban civilizations. The sacred was withdrawn from nature, but now it was met in the conventions of society. In the situation of the Israelites, the sacred rested in the decalogue, the ritual laws, and the covenant. The worth of the individual was derived from society and its structure. This phase was due to the rise of rational thinking. The intensified capacity for rational thought is evidenced in the careful planning engaged in by society. As a transitional phase, mythical thinking and rational thinking were highly mixed. In all developments of consciousness there is a conjunction of an inner readiness in the human psyche and external pressures which demand psychic adaptation. For example, the domestication of animals, the cultivation of plants, and the emergence of great cities sometime in the fourth millennium B.C. required great planning, which in turn probably stimulated an increased rational ability.

The "post-conventional" or "axial" phase of consciousness is located sometime in the first millennium B.C. up to approximately 500 A.D. In this axial period rational thinking emerged over mythical thinking and reason became the basis for the new consciousness. For the first time, human consciousness, properly so called, is evident. Self-reflection saw in personhood a core of autonomy and freedom. Free and autonomous individuals could control themselves and respect their inherent worth. The individuated person became a possibility.

This axial phase of consciousness is the most significant phase for the Judaeo-Christian tradition. Just as the conventional phase saw a distancing from the dominance of nature, the axial phase resulted in a distancing from the dominance of societal structures. Certain prophets, having a new sense of what it means to be an individual, criticized the conventional consciousness. Jeremiah, in particular, is a leading figure in axial consciousness. His sense of a unique selfhood is seen in portions of his writings which are like a spiritual autobiography. He places salvation not in a restored society but in full personal individuality and self-responsibility.

Israel was enabled to enter an axial consciousness through its increasingly rational understanding of God. Other societies, at the same time, emerged into axial consciousness but the Israelite development was distinct because it was viewed as a response to a God who summons to a personal mode of existence. Gradually, in the faith of Israel, reality itself was seen as grace.

Jesus completed the breakthrough into axial consciousness begun in the prophets. His life, death, and resurrection provided a new basis for understanding the radical nature of the call to personhood. The resurrection belief of the Christian community demonstrated a qualitatively new level of consciousness within axial consciousness.

The prophets had gradually discovered the transcendent God who was beyond nature and society. In their radical monotheism they discovered themselves called into individuated existence by this God. The belief in God nurtured an understanding of the human as transcending physical and biological limits. The spiritual nature of the self slowly became clear.

Resurrection belief signaled an awareness of the radical form of individuation now possible for people. This new consciousness in Christians allowed for a confidence in a divine presence which eliminates any barriers to human autonomy and freedom. As William Thompson expresses it:

> The resurrection belief rightly conjures up in the human imagination the image of the fulfilled man who has conquered all forces threatening to destroy human individuation. That this belief became the central belief in Christianity argues for the emergence in Christianity of a psyche that believed itself capable of full human individuation. Such a psyche could not have emerged unless it experienced the presence of a transcendent spiritual source, co-constituting its very self, empowering it to transcend all forces threatening to destroy the self.[45]

Between the thirteenth and seventeenth centuries A.D. an additional development of axial consciousness began to emerge in the form of historical consciousness. In particular the Renaissance and the Enlightenment opened up a new understanding of time and the role humans play as the creators of their own history. Along with the awareness of one's individuality which was fostered by axial consciousness, historical consciousness brought the insight that each individual is a free and active cause, a self-creative subject.

Thompson points to the spiritual literature of the sixteenth century, especially the writings of Martin Luther, Ignatius Loyola, and Teresa of Avila, as indications of a growing historical consciousness. Ignatius and Teresa analyze spiritual development from a subjective point of view. The spiritual life is not simply something which happens to a person but is a process which a person actively enters into in a free response to God.

Today our phase of human development is seen as a time of historical consciousness. We are more and more aware of the historically-conditioned nature of all things human, including religion. It is a time of rich possibilities for Christianity as it explores the foundations of its tradition and leans to speak to and from a contemporary consciousness.

A danger which Thompson sees in today's situation is what

he calls the problem of the "isolated ego." With the stress on individuality and self-creativity the autonomous individual can become lonely and isolated. The heightened emphasis on reflection and analysis can lead in the direction of self-mastery, self-control.

A Jungian perspective enters Thompson's analysis at this point. He finds himself in agreement with the Jungian analyst Erich Neumann who warns of the danger of over-emphasizing the conscious part of the psyche. Neumann speaks of the now familiar negative outcomes of such a situation. Either the unconscious will erupt and the individual will be inflated and identify with the forces of the unconscious, or there will be such a divorce from the unconscious that ego-consciousness will substitute intellect and thinking for the life of the whole psyche. Neumann refers to the latter state as a "sclerosis of consciousness." Thompson believes it is instructive for Christians to read these words of the Jungian Neumann: "A good example of this is the concept of God, which now derives wholly from the sphere of consciousness—or purports to derive from it, as the ego is deluded enough to pretend. There is no longer anything transpersonal, but only personal; there are no more archetypes, but only concepts; no more symbols, only signs."[46]

The Interior Castle and Christian Individuation

The preceding analysis of the development of human consciousness, and the relationship of Christ to that development, lends support to the psychological, symbolical approach we have been taking to *The Interior Castle*. And it provides a context for further reflection upon Teresa's writing.

The Interior Castle is a work of axial, historical consciousness. It is an intensely interior document plunging the reader into the core of human personality. Pre-conventional consciousness is left behind as the individual rejects outer identifications, withdraws projections, and begins to explore an inner world. Conventional consciousness, too, with its emphasis on conformity to societal structures, gives way to an axial consciousness which locates the sacred in the numinous depths of the person. The individual on the journey realizes the need to become self-creative, to enter actively into the process, to learn to freely let go and open oneself to the center. This accent on individual responsibility for the journey is indicative of historical consciousness.

Teresa presents a program which recognizes the problem of the "isolated ego." The ego is isolated as long as the depths of the self are unplumbed. She realizes that self-control and self-mastery only heighten the sense of alienation when they become defenses for the threatened ego. Her program encourages a letting-go of one's tight control on life and entry into the riches of an unsuspected world which is available to the adventurous of heart. The alternatives are not between a stable ego-isolation and an unstable, disruptive movement into the unknown. Ego-isolation itself, in time, becomes an untenable situation and leads to instability and possible collapse and disintegration. Teresa warns us that the journey into life, into reality, once begun, must continue. We either enter into reality freely and creatively, or we are dragged into it, and perhaps dragged under by it. Even the good Christian of the third dwelling place must continue on pilgrimage in life, learning further to give way to reality.

This reality is experienced as graced by a divine presence. The movement into personhood in *The Interior Castle* is a response to a divine call. The free, autonomous person emerges as the relationship with God deepens.

In Teresa's journey in prayer, the deepening relationship with God is accompanied by the emergence of the figure of Christ in the latter dwelling places. This divine image not only expresses the growing intimacy with God, but also, as a psychological symbol, signals the emergence of a more completely individuated personality, a fuller realization of the self.

Teresa's emphasis on the imitation of Christ in his suffering springs from a Christian faith which has learned to fully enter into life with a radical trust in God. As William Thompson expresses it: "In this Christian notion of individuation, the ego or self is not annulled, but co-exists simultaneously with and comes to fulfillment because of the personalized presence of God."[47] Central to this trust is the experience of the followers of Jesus whose qualitatively new consciousness and resurrection belief were generated by the experience of the risen Lord.

The serpents of the castle are descendants of the dinosaurs of a pre-conventional, pre-conscious phase of psychic life. The powers of the unconscious which once engulfed our ancestors are still very much with us. The serpents remind us of the fragility of consciousness. They warn us of the dangers of identifying with the collective consciousness around us as well as being trapped by the collective unconscious within us.

Teresa's approach is not to identify with nature, but to let creation speak of its maker. Her symbolic approach allows her to freely and creatively respond to the mystery which reveals itself in her life. Her symbolic images in *The Interior Castle* speak of a movement away from the darkness of an alienated, constricted psychic life on the periphery. Responding to the call from the center, the pilgrim undergoes a series of transformations of awareness in the dwelling places leading to the experience of oneness with the ultimate source of light and personal identity.

Not only is pre-conventional, mythic thinking replaced by conscious, symbolic contemplation, but conventional consciousness too is renewed. Instead of a relationship to society which was basically one of conformity, the individuated Christian realizes her unity with, and responsibility to, her brothers and sisters. The sign of union with God does not lie in ecstatic phenomena but in the quality of reflective consciousness and humane service which characterize a Christian. The seventh dwelling place demonstrates such a consciousness with its concern for service.

Furthermore, the fully individuated Christian dwelling in the center of the castle gives promise of a future Christian consciousness which is transcultural. An historical consciousness assists us in understanding that a particular cultural form of Christianity is not the only or final expression of Christianity. For example, an historical consciousness allows us to appropriate Teresa's teaching on prayer and the spiritual life without at the same time identifying the fullest expression of that life with sixteenth-century Spanish Christendom. Again in William

Thompson's words, "The truly autonomous Christian has simply developed his individuation 'to full ripeness' and thereby discovered his real freedom from every partial aspect of the self: family, society, position, or culture."[48]

The increasing interaction of peoples and religions points to further developments in axial consciousness. The individuated Christian will be one who is open to a dialogue with the world in the expectation of being transformed by the experience. Jung learned that all life was a circumambulation of the center. No one resided at the center. Even in Teresa's castle the experience of the center is relative. God continues to call from the center of existence, and human consciousness continues to unfold in new transformations. In the future, individuated Christians will be living into the fuller implications of Christ's life, death, and resurrection, just as they will be living into the unknown regions of the self symbolized in Christ.

Concluding Reflections and Suggestions

The final image of our study has been the image of Christ. We have noted the occurrences of this image in the visionary experiences of Teresa. And we have listened to her reflections on the following of Christ. Carl Jung's psychological probings of the Christ symbol were presented, along with his concern for a missing shadow dimension in Christ. The image of the crucified Christ was offered as a particularly absorbing symbol of the self, and the individuation process was viewed in terms of a crucifixion.

Next, we looked at the development of consciousness in the broad sweep of historical ages. Christ's role in radicalizing that development again showed the pivotal position of Christ in relationship to the human psyche, historically and in contemporary consciousness.

From this perspective, *The Interior Castle* was reaffirmed as a document of Christian individuation. It is a testimony to the emergence of full personhood in response to a transcendent God experienced within the human personality. This divine presence does not annul but summons forth the human person. The Christ event in history made possible this full, axial, historical consciousness found in *The Interior Castle*. And Christ today, one with the Father and present to contemporary consciousness, energizes the Christian for fullness of life in an individuated existence.

It is fitting to end this exploration of symbols of *The Interior Castle* with the symbol of Christ. Not only is union with Christ a goal of Teresa's journey through the castle, but Christ and the symbols of religion were a major preoccupation in the life and work of Carl Jung. Beginning with a childhood dream of a phallic divinity and continuing through reflections on God by an elderly Jung in his autobiography, religious questions were never far from his concerns.

"I find that all my thoughts," he wrote, "circle around God like the planets around the sun, and are as irresistibly attracted by Him. I would feel it to be the grossest sin if I were to oppose any resistance to this force."[49]

At times, of course, it is difficult to understand just what Jung thinks about God and Christianity. He studied the phenomenon of religion from such non-traditional viewpoints, and he wrote so much about religion over the years, that it is possible to find almost any attitude toward religion documented in his writings. On the balance, however, it would be difficult to say that he simply psychologized religion. It would be fair to say that he attempted to show the psychic roots of religion and the psychic relevance of Christianity. And his work was no mere intellectual exercise. He was trying to understand the deepest movements of his own psyche.

If we say of Jung that he does not demonstrate the certitude of faith which we would expect in a truly religious person, he might say of the complacent or defensive Christian that such a person's faith is stuck in unexamined assumptions. Besides, it is getting late in the day for Christianity to disregard new understandings which might build bridges to contemporary men and women.

I have always found this statement of Jung's a helpful clari-
fication of his project:

> I am not . . . addressing myself to the happy possessors
> of faith, but to those many people for whom the light
> has gone out, the mystery has faded, and God is dead.
> For most of them there is no going back, and one does
> not know either whether going back is always the bet-
> ter way. To gain an understanding of religious matters,
> probably all that is left us today is the psychological ap-
> proach. That is why I take these thought-forms that
> have become historically fixed, try to melt them down
> again and pour them into moulds of immediate experi-
> ence. It is certainly a difficult undertaking to discover
> connecting links between dogma and immediate expe-
> rience of psychological archetypes, but a study of the
> natural symbols of the unconscious gives us the neces-
> sary raw material.[50]

And in another place he writes:

> The fact is that with the knowledge and actual experi-
> ence of these inner images a way is opened for reason
> and feeling to gain access to those other images which
> the teachings of religion offer to mankind. Psychology
> thus does just the opposite of what it is accused of: it
> provides possible approaches to a better understanding
> of these things, it opens people's eyes to the real mean-
> ing of dogmas, and, far from destroying, it throws open
> an empty house to new inhabitants.[51]

The above words of Jung indicate the spirit in which this
study of the images of *The Interior Castle* was undertaken. In a
time of shifting consciousness and the disappearance of Christendom as a cultural package, the traditions of Christianity need
to be re-examined in the light of our present experience and un-

derstanding. In particular, the mystical tradition, as exemplified in Teresa of Avila, is a rich source for a deeper appreciation of human interiority. Far from being relegated to the museums of the world, Christianity has the potential to speak to contemporary minds and even to invite and anticipate future worlds of meaning.

It often seems to be the case that intense preoccupation with the mystery of existence results in a vital life but few answers. Jung was willing to call the mystery at the center of life "God" because by doing so, he said, we are naming the unknown by the more unknown. He did not consider himself as one possessing answers. In the last pages of his autobiography we find him saying:

> The older I have become, the less I have understood or had insight into or known about myself. . . . There is nothing I am quite sure about. . . . I exist on the foundation of something I do not know. In spite of all uncertainties, I feel a solidity underlying all existence and a continuity in my mode of being. . . .
>
> . . . The archetype of the old man who has seen enough is eternally true. . . . Yet there is so much that fills me: plants, animals, clouds, day and night, and the eternal in man. The more uncertain I have felt about myself, the more there has grown up in me a feeling of kinship with all things.[52]

An insightful student of the psyche in her own way, Teresa of Avila would have sympathized with Jung's difficulties in comprehending the paradoxes of life. As with Jung's theory of the individuation process, Teresa's clear structure of a castle with its seven dwelling places provides only the barest semblance of order for experiences which she often found inexpressible. Teresa searched for images and words with which to convey the subtleties of the inner world to which God called her. Her images were symbols hinting at transformations born of her relationship with God. She had a difficult task in writing

The Interior Castle, and in its final lines, a closing prayer, she admits her confusion:

> May it please His Majesty, my Sisters and daughters, that we all reach that place where we may ever praise Him. Through the merits of His Son who lives and reigns forever and ever, may He give me the grace to carry out something of what I tell you, amen. For I tell you that my confusion is great, and thus I ask you through the same Lord that in your prayers you do not forget this poor wretch.[53]

If two intensely reflective and searching lives end in admissions of uncertainty, we may take heart in our own insecurities. Teresa and Jung have provided us with some answers. Teresa tells us that the radical foundation on which we build our lives is a divine presence in those lives. And Jung describes flesh and blood developments we may expect as we move toward the self. But, perhaps most strikingly, they both offer us the example of courageous pilgrims who trustingly give themselves over to a journey to the sacred in life.

NOTES

1. Jung, C.W., XII, 11.
2. Jung, C.W. XII, 20.
3. Jung, C.W., XI, 137.
4. Jung, C.W., XII, 20.
5. Jung, C.W., XI, 238.
6. Jung, C.W., IXii, 170.
7. Jung, C.W., XII, 22.
8. Jung, C.W., IXii, 69, 70.
9. Jung, C.W., IXii, 122.
10. *Interior Castle,* VI, chap. 8, no. 1.
11. Ibid., VI, chap. 8, no. 2.
12. Ibid., VI, chap. 9, no. 3.
13. Ibid., VI, chap. 9, no. 4.

14. Ibid., VI, chap. 9, no. 12.
15. Ibid., VII, chap. 2, no. 2.
16. Ibid., VII, chap. 2, no. 1.
17. Ibid.
18. Ibid., VII, chap. 2, no. 3.
19. Ibid., VII, chap. 2, no. 5.
20. Ibid., VII, chap. 4, no. 4.
21. Ibid., VII, chap. 4, no. 8.
22. Jung, C.W., XI, 232.
23. Jung, C.W., IXii, 74.
24. Jung, C.W., IXii, 75.
25. Jung, C.W., IXii, 84.
26. Cf. David Burrell, *Exercises in Religious Understanding* (University of Notre Dame Press, 1974), pp. 222-231; Victor White, *Soul and Psyche* (New York: Harper and Brothers, 1960), pp. 141-165.
27. *Interior Castle*, VII, chap. 4, no. 8.
28. Ibid., VII, chap. 4, no. 4
29. Jung, C.W., IXii, 79.
30. Jung, C.W., XI, 233.
31. Edinger, *Ego and Archetype*, p. 152.
32. Sebastian Moore, *The Crucified Jesus Is No Stranger* (New York: The Seabury Press, A Crossroad Book, 1977), p. 7.
33. Ibid., p. 105.
34. Ibid., p. 11.
35. Ibid., p. x.
36. Ibid., p. 19.
37. Ibid., p. 91.
38. Ibid., p. 30.
39. Ibid., p. 42.
40. *Interior Castle*, VII, chap. 4, no. 4.
41. Jung, C.W., XII, 7.
42. Jung, C.W., XII, 7.
43. Jung, C.W., XI, 233.
44. William Thompson, *Christ and Consciousness* (New York: Paulist Press, 1977). Thompson lists among his major sources Karl Jaspers, John Cobb, and Eric Voegelin.
45. Ibid., 71.
46. Ibid., 125.
47. Ibid., 183.
48. Ibid., 150.

49. Jung, *Memories*, p. xi.
50. Jung, C.W., XI, 148.
51. Jung, C.W., XII, 17.
52. Jung, *Memories*, p. 359.
53. *Interior Castle*, VII, chap. 4, no. 16.

CONCLUSION

Through the Castle, One More Time

Above all, Teresa of Avila's *The Interior Castle* is meant to be an encouragement and a guide in the living of a life more and more centered on God. In encouraging the reader to enter an inner world, Teresa is inviting us to walk around the meanings of our life. She is giving us a free and protected space in which to become playful pilgrims on our way to our center. As we enter within ourselves we reflectively engage our lives and listen for God's call.

Carl Jung tells us that we meet ourselves in a thousand different disguises on the road of life. Our pilgrimage winds among the images of our life. These images are revealed in our feelings, found in the night in our dream-figures, and discovered in the people and places of our surrounding world. Each engaging image becomes a window to our depths and a wayside shrine on our pilgrimage.

The castle image urges us to attend to our symbols of wholeness. Who or what symbolizes my self, the fullness of life which I desire? What in life engages me in the core of my being? When and where do I feel most at home? Our images can be identified and reflected upon for the challenge they may contain.

At first, our journey seems to be of our own initiative. But more and more it is evident that we are responding to a centering process which is introducing us to worlds within. We are aware of a presence in our life.

The waters within are deep, the repository of vessels waiting to be raised and numbered among the treasures of our life. Moving in this realm immerses us in a timeless, collective fluid which links us with our sources and with all life. The waters of the castle are restorative for us, healing our brokenness.

The brokenness is the result of a previous journey, a migration out of the collective waters toward an independent existence. We moved into the world to gain a basic identity, to test our skills, to find our role. It was the morning of life. Jung reminds us that the rules are different in the afternoon. Instead of gaining more control, we need to let go and be receptive. Instead of resting in our security, we are called to continue the journey, but now by an inner road. We have to reconstellate the self that was lost when we set out to conquer the world.

The first figure we meet on the inner journey is barely recognizable. It is part of the self we have been avoiding, a shadow figure living animal-like out in the forests. Not willing to own it ourselves we have given our shadow to others to carry for us. We can be disgusted and judgmental because it is somebody else's problem. We do not recognize the part of our personality we are ashamed to own.

To be confronted by this figure demanding recognition is enough to abruptly halt the journey. We would be tempted to go back and to vow never to be this adventuresome again. Confronting the shadow requires not only a recognition but an experiencing of our destructive possibilities. It is a felt knowledge which shakes us.

We cannot circumvent the shadow. In time we learn to own and care for this apparently pathetic part of ourselves. But in the experience we find that owning our shadow does not diminish us. In fact, the shadow, now given acceptance and a warm place near the hearth, becomes a new source of life for us. We discover what Jung, too, learned: the shadow is ninety percent gold. The serpents and devils of Teresa's castle become valued inhabitants.

As the inner journey continues we learn again and again

that the paschal mystery will be experienced in our own lives. The cross comes before any resurrection. The psychologist Jung warned that there is no new consciousness without pain and confusion. Teresa showed that the butterfly required a preparation time in an envelope of darkness.

Our crises can lead to transformations and conversions. We find a strength within us, and yet beyond us, which heals the wounded psyche and continues our journey of centering. Jung found in the human psyche a mystery that healed. Teresa said it was a matter of continuing to hear God's call and allowing that call to guide us through the valleys and windings of the journey.

We learn that the darkness in life does not have to win. The pilgrimage is renewed after each experience of night. But we are not the same. The night has done its work. The log has been scorched as it slowly becomes one with the flame. Something has died and we have grieved. But something else has been born and we are now filled with that new life.

Far regions of the psyche are penetrated. Their strange otherness finds symbolization in masculine and feminine figures. We experience ourselves in our outer limits. At these limits Teresa tells us that we touch God and our masculine and feminine images marry in the coming to be of our self-for-God.

In our relationships, especially in the mysterious relationship between man and woman, we reach beyond ourselves to the unknown other. Teresa reveals that we are reaching for the transcendent God. All our marriages are between the known and the unknown, between us and God.

Christ teaches us to trust this movement to the center. He encourages and empowers us to let go and be drawn, through our experiences, to God. Christ, in his death and resurrection, is a guarantee that our journey to the center of the castle brings fullness of life in union with God.

SELECTED BIBLIOGRAPHY

Texts

1. Carl Jung

Jung, C. G. *Collected Works.* Translated by R. F. C. Hull. Edited by Sir Herbert Read et al. 20 Vols. Bollingen Series XX. Princeton, N.J.: Princeton University Press, 1953–1979.
———. *Letters.* Vol. 1: 1906–1950. Princeton, N.J.: Princeton University Press, 1973.
———. *Letters.* Vol. 2: 1951–1961. Princeton, N.J.: Princeton University Press, 1975.
———. *Memories, Dreams, Reflections.* New York: Pantheon Books, 1963.
———. *Visions Seminars.* 2 Vols. Notes of Mary Foote. Zurich: Spring Publications, 1976.

2. Teresa of Avila

The Collected Works of St. Teresa of Avila. Translated by Kieran Kavanaugh and Otilio Rodriguez. Vol. 1: *The Book of Her Life, Spiritual Testimonies, Soliloquies.* Washington, D.C.: Institute of Carmelite Studies, 1976. Vol. 2: *The Way of Perfection, Meditations on The Song of Songs, The Interior Castle.* Washington, D.C.: Institute of Carmelite Studies, 1980.
The Complete Works of St. Teresa of Jesus. Translated and edited by E. Allison Peers. New York: Sheed and Ward, 1946.
Teresa of Avila. *The Interior Castle.* Translated by Kieran Kavanaugh and Otilio Rodriguez. New York: Paulist Press, 1979.

Biographical Studies

1. Carl Jung

Brome, Vincent. *Jung.* New York: Atheneum, 1978.
van der Post, Laurens. *Jung and The Story of Our Time.* New York: Pantheon Books, 1975.

2. Teresa of Avila

Auclair, M. *Teresa of Avila.* Translated by Kathleen Pond. New York: Pantheon Books, Inc., 1953.
Clissold, Stephen. *St. Teresa of Avila.* London: Sheldon Press, 1979.
Efren de la Madre De Dios and Otger Steggink. *Tiempo Y Vida De Santa Teresa.* Madrid: Biblioteca De Autores Cristianos, 1977.
Smet, Joachim. *The Carmelites.* Vol. 2. Darien, Ill.: Carmelite Spiritual Center, 1976.

Studies

1. Carl Jung

Edinger, Edward. *Ego and Archetype.* Baltimore: Penguin Books, Inc., 1973.
Heisig, James. *Imago Dei: A Study of C. G. Jung's Psychology of Religion.* Lewisburg: Bucknell University Press, 1979.
Homans, Peter. *Jung in Context.* Chicago: University of Chicago Press, 1979.
Jacobi, Jolande. *The Psychology of C. G. Jung.* New Haven: Yale University Press, 1943.
Progoff, Ira. *Jung's Psychology and Its Social Meaning.* Garden City, New York: Anchor Books, 1973.
Singer, June. *Boundaries of the Soul.* Garden City, New York: Doubleday and Company, Inc., 1972.
Whitmont, Edward. *The Symbolic Quest.* New York: Harper and Row, 1973.

2. Teresa of Avila

Burrows, Ruth. *Fire Upon the Earth: Interior Castle Explored.* Denville, N.J.: Dimension Books, 1981.

Dicken, E. W. Trueman. *The Crucible of Love.* New York: Sheed and Ward, 1963.

Hatzfeld, Helmut A. *Santa Teresa De Avila.* New York: Twayne Publishers, Inc., 1969.

Marie-Eugene de l'Enfant Jesus. *I Want To See God.* Translated by Sister M. Verda Clare. Chicago: Fides, 1953.

—————. *I Am a Daughter of the Church.* Translated by Sister M. Verda Clare. Chicago: Fides, 1955.

INDEX